# Your Child at Play:
# One to Two Years

# Your Child at Play: One to Two Years

*Dr. Marilyn Segal*
*and*
*Dr. Don Adcock*

**Newmarket Press**
**New York**

To my parents, for their optimism and hope

Copyright © 1985 Marilyn Segal, Ph.D., and Don Adcock, Ph.D.
A Mailman Family Press book published by Newmarket Press, drawn from research conducted at Nova University, Ft. Lauderdale, Florida.
This book published simultaneously in the United States of America and in Canada.

2  3  4  5  6  7  8  9  0  F/C
            9  0  F/P

**Library of Congress Cataloging in Publication Data**

Segal, Marilyn M.
  Your child at play: one to two years.

  Bibliography: p.
  Includes index.
  1. Child rearing.   2. Child development.   3. Play.
4. Learning.   5. Creative activities and seat work.
I. Adcock, Don.   II. Title.
HQ767.9.S425   1985      649'.122      84-14318
ISBN 0-937858-52-8
ISBN 0-937858-53-6 (pbk.)

The author gratefully acknowledges the continuing grant from the A. L. Mailman Family Foundation, Inc., which supported the writing of this book.

Volumes in the *Your Child at Play* series:
   *Your Child at Play: Birth to One Year*
   *Your Child at Play: One to Two Years*
   *Your Child at Play: Two to Three Years*
   *Your Child at Play: Three to Five Years*
Published simultaneously in hardcover and paperback editions

*Quantity Purchases*
*Companies, professional groups, clubs, and other organizations may qualify for special terms when ordering quantities of this title. For information, contact the Special Sales Department, Newmarket Press, 18 East 48th Street, New York, New York 10017. Phone (212) 832-3575.*

Manufactured in the United States of America

# Table of Contents

# Overview

Nicholas, 20 months, was sitting on his cousin's tricycle protesting loudly because the pedals would not turn. When his Dad leaned over to give him a helpful push, his protests grew even louder. Nicholas did not want help with this tricycle. He wanted to ride it himself.

Taking care of a child between one and two years old is an exciting experience. The toddler year is a period of self-definition. Children, like Nicholas, are discovering that they are distinct individuals with the ability to manage things on their own  and make other people do their bidding. As they explore their own capabilities, they are bound to meet frustration. Upset and out of sorts, they inevitably send messages to the adults around them. "Leave me alone, I can do it myself!" "Help, I'm having trouble!"

*One to Two Years* is a practical guide for parents who are faced with the everyday challenges of living with a toddler. Based on information collected from hundreds of families, it includes suggestions, strategies and activities for managing problem situations and increasing the fun of parent-toddler play. Although *One to Two Years* is a sequel to *Birth to One Year*, it does not follow the same month-by-month sequential format. Because toddlers have different rates and patterns of development, the book is organized according to topics rather than age. The first section, "Exploration," looks at ways in which toddlers explore their environment: touching objects, emptying and filling, and practicing new motor skills. The second section, "Everyday Living," describes daily routines, going out in public, and attempting to help with grown-up jobs. The final section, "Playing and Learning," explores the learning that takes place in different kinds of play.

Within every chapter of *One to Two Years*, the authors talk about competing objectives. How can parents and caregivers encourage independence and still help children accept reasonable limits and follow rules? How can they take advantage of a child's ability to learn without creating pressure or taking the fun out of play? Despite our practical orientation, we do not offer precise solutions to such dilemmas. Striking a balance between competing objectives (which is the rule rather than the exception) is ultimately up to the parent. What we try to do in this book is to outline a number of alternatives. The greater the range of options, the easier it will be to translate parental values into practical terms.

It is our firm belief that the study of child development can never scientifically reveal one approach that is best for children. We have seen one-year olds flourish in many different family settings with different styles of caregiving. Our intent is to supplement parental experience, to enlarge the scope of professional inquiry, and to enrich the dialogue concerning the way we care for our young children.

# *Part I*
# EXPLORATION

# Introduction

| | |
|---|---|
| Mother: | (Looking into a baby carriage as she holds her toddler by the hand.) |
| | "What an adorable baby! What beautiful big blue eyes! Terry, see the pretty baby." |
| Terry: | (Reaching into the carriage and poking at the baby's face.) |
| | "Eyes—baby eyes." |
| Mother: | "Be gentle, Terry. Just touch the baby's hand. We don't want to hurt the baby." |

As we watch this brief scene, we realize how much of a difference there is between taking care of a baby and taking care of a toddler. In the first year of life, parents are concerned with understanding their baby's cues and meeting their baby's needs. Beginning in the toddler year, parents change their focus. Major emphasis is now placed on helping children become more self-sufficient and responsible. No longer are parents satisfied with doing everything for their children. Instead, they begin to encourage the children to explore their own surroundings and discover their own capacities.

It has been said time and again that you have to be young to be a parent. This saying really strikes home in the toddler year. From morning to night,

the typical toddler is on the go and into everything in sight. On the positive side, the child is a great companion, enthusiastic, vital and excited by each new discovery. On the problem side, an energetic and curious youngster requires constant watching. Realistically, parents do have to say "no" to their toddlers. At the same time, they need to recognize that the meaning a toddler attaches to "no" can have long-term significance. If children hear the word "no" too often, they may think that "no" means "don't try, don't find out."

As parents adapt to the exploration of a one-year old, they find themselves facing new emotions. During the first year, they smiled indulgently when their baby crawled over to the coffee table and gingerly touched the leaves of a plant. Now, when the child pulls the plant off the coffee table and breaks it, parents hear themselves responding with a strong and angry "no." Just as toddlers need time to learn the rules about exploration, parents of one-year olds need time to deal with negative feelings and adjust to their expanded role.

The first section of this book is devoted to issues that are related to exploration. In Chapter 1, "Hands on Everything," we discuss how you can respond to your toddler's desire to handle all kinds of objects. In Chapter 2,

"Emptying and Filling," we look at how you can guide your toddler through the stage of emptying and filling containers and rearranging the house. In Chapter 3, "New Muscle Power," we describe how parents can both encourage and protect their children as they practice new physical skills. Throughout these three chapters, there is a common theme: how parents can encourage exploration while still keeping it within bounds. Finally, in the last chapter of Section One, we look at some ways through which parents can help children overcome fears that may arise in conjunction with exploration.

# Chapter 1
# HANDS ON
# EVERYTHING

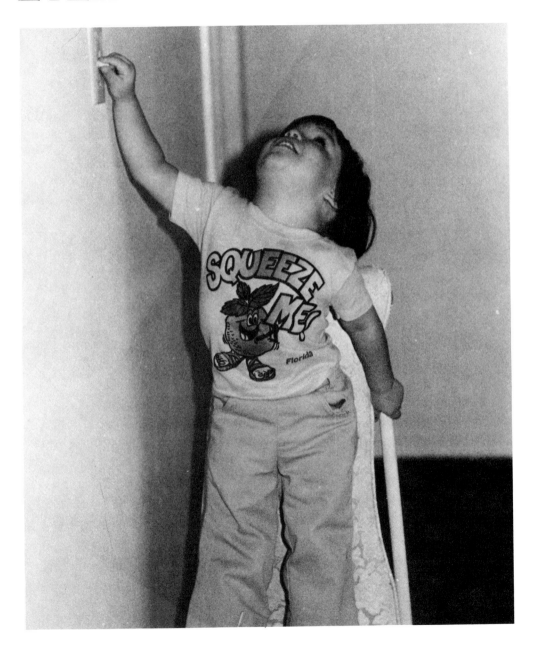

The Scene: The living room in Grandma's house.

Mother: "Now that this granddaughter of yours has learned to walk, she's into everything."

Grandma: "It's okay. There's not a thing in here she could break. Just put her down and let her play."

A FEW SECONDS LATER:

Mother: "Oh dear, Amelia just pulled on the tablecloth and knocked that flower vase on the floor."

Grandma: "Mmm—oh, well. It wasn't that valuable anyway." (Smiling and holding Amelia in the air.) "You are a little lightening bolt, aren't you? I'm just glad that you didn't get hurt. Now, let's see if we can find some toys for you."

Young toddlers, as Amelia's grandmother learned soon enough, are busy, delightful little people who cannot always be trusted. Left on their own in a room full of interesting objects, their agenda is investigation. Figurines on the coffee table may be examined one by one, television knobs twisted and pulled, vases and flower pots turned upside down. The children are not trying to be naughty. They simply are very curious and their way of learning about things is a "hands on" approach.

Touching is not this much of a problem with all one-year olds, of course. Some children, after a cursory investigation of household objects, decide that toys and people are more interesting. Even toddlers who tend to leave things alone however, are tempted to touch in a new situation. A delicate Christmas ornament, a crystal candy dish, or a bowl of artificial fruit can spark their interest. Sooner or later, all parents of one to two-year olds are faced with the challenge of limiting exploration while at the same time supporting their child's healthy curiosity.

In actuality, the guidelines for touching and not touching objects are rather complicated. Some objects can never be touched, some objects can be touched all the time, and some objects can be touched only when a grownup is around to supervise. Objects that appear to be similar have to be treated differently. A wind-up musical toy can be treated roughly, but Grandma's antique

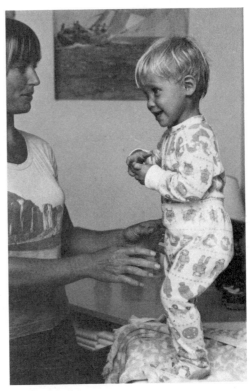

music box cannot be picked up at all. The string of beads from Mother's top drawer can be dragged around the house, but the beads that she keeps in her jewelry box are permanently off limits. Picking the leaves off houseplants is forbidden, but pulling weeds out of the garden is a way of being helpful. It is understandable that toddlers need a good measure of time and guidance in order to discriminate between these different situations.

# Rules About Touching

In most homes, parents keep dangerous objects like sharp knives, medicines and detergents out of a toddler's reach. But even in the best child-proofed homes, there are many "don't touch" objects. In the bathroom, for example, a major attraction is the toilet bowl. In the kitchen there is a refrigerator and a garbage container. In the living room, expensive stereo systems, antiques and valuable books are usually off limits.

At first, parents may try to keep toddlers away from these objects by closing doors or putting up barriers. Parents who use this technique, however, report mixed results. Keeping the door closed is effective with a room that is seldom used, such as the parents' bedroom. But when the door is frequently opened and closed, toddlers become aware of the parent's strategy and work hard to beat the system. As Brian's mother put it, "My son has a sixth sense. The one time out of a hundred I forget to close that bathroom door, he's in there splashing in the toilet."

After a while, most parents decide that it is easier to teach toddlers some "don't touch" rules than to spend their day playing guard. One of the simplest ways to keep children from handling off-limit objects is to provide alternatives. Anton's father told us his son was "into everything," the silverware drawer in the kitchen, the record cabinet in the living room, and the linen closet in the bathroom. In the kitchen, the problem was at least partially solved by setting aside two drawers for Anton. In the living room, a lower shelf was reserved for objects that were safe to handle. Even in the bathroom, unrestricted exploration was allowed in one small drawer.

 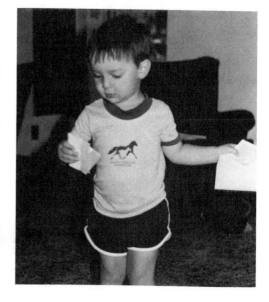

Parents who use the "special drawer strategy" offer the following suggestion. Rather than placing toys in the child's drawer or cabinet, put in "adult" objects. In the kitchen cabinet, for instance, put a couple of pots with lids, a sponge, a wooden spoon, a coffee perculator, and a strainer. In the family room, fill a desk drawer with junk mail, old magazines, and an outdated TV guide. Then change these adult objects on a regular basis, removing items that are no longer of interest and substituting new ones that pose greater challenge.

No matter how cleverly parents provide substitute objects or divert exploration to acceptable locations, there will be times when a child has to be reminded that an object is off limits. In these situations, the most effective restraint is a verbal message. Children are sensitive to tone of voice and will respond to a single word like "hot" or "sharp." In fact, the children often begin to remind others about "don't touch" rule. Allison, at fourteen months, was aware that ashes were not to be played in. Whenever a visitor used an ashtray, she would hold her finger over the ashtray and declare in a solemn voice, "dirty." Such one word messages, which are variations on the theme of "no," give children an inkling why exploration is not permitted. As one-year olds become better able to understand language, parents can reinforce their rules with more complicated explanations. They can begin to talk about objects belonging to someone else or about objects being breakable.

When parents are available to oversee a one-year old's play, rules about touching are often bent or relaxed. Telephones, for example, can be played with when a parent is nearby to check on random dialing. When no one is around, one-year olds are not supposed to handle the phone. As parents monitor exploration, they also model the appropriate way to handle objects. Under guidance, one-year olds may be permitted to experiment with butter knives, ballpoint pens and stereo knobs.

Demonstration and verbal guidance can be used to teach one-year olds how to handle delicate objects as well. Instead of saying "no" or "don't touch," parents are able to use worlds like, "touch gently," "make nice," "let's carry it together," or "we have to be careful." Tina's mother took advantage of the fact that Tina liked to point at objects. She taught Tina how to touch delicate objects with an extended forefinger, as if she were pointing at them. Soon Tina understood that the phrase "just touch" meant that her exploration was limited to this special kind of pointing. David's father used a similar verbal prompt with his son, who was in the habit of sticking his fingers into their dachshund's eyes. "Make nice Corky," he explained, as he showed his son how to pat the dog softly on the head.

A logical extension of "touch gently" is "hold it carefully." Having identified the fact that certain objects require special handling, the one-to two-

year old is ready to take on the greater challenge of holding a delicate object. At first you will want to show your child how to hold the object while standing still. After a while, your child will learn to carry an object from one

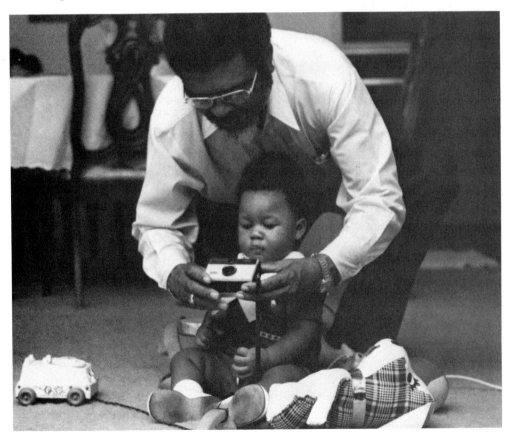

spot to the next, putting it down very gently. Parents who have not risked this kind of teaching are often surprised at how trustworthy toddlers are when they are given the opportunity to learn.

When teaching children how to handle objects carefully, it is especially important to phrase explanations in a positive way. Rather than saying, "Be careful not to rip the pages," you can say to a child, "Turn the pages gently—it is such a pretty book." Rather than saying, "Don't crush the flower," you can say, "Touch the flower with your finger. It is very delicate." Finding verbal explanations that are simple enough to be understood is not easy, of course, but it is well worth the effort. With every explanation, you stimulate language development and let your child learn through exploration.

## A Last Resort

In all families there are times when one year old children have trouble accepting the rules parents have set. If children are first learning a rule, parents are usually content to remind them about infractions. With young toddlers, parents may try to distract them by picking them up and moving them to a different spot. Older toddlers can sometimes be distracted from a forbidden object by trading it with an alternative object.

When children persist in violating a rule, however, parents look for stronger measures. They find that their options are limited. A toddler who disobeys a rule about touching can be yelled at, spanked, or restrained by "time-out" from a play situation. We believe the latter choice is preferable for two reasons. First, it is more logical. If a one-year old keeps getting into something that is off limits, it makes sense that the consequence be a temporary restriction of exploration. Second, a time-out situation does not hurt or demean young children. Time-out, which can be as simple as holding a child's hand and saying "just look," does not frighten a child. If the damage is done before the parent arrives on the scene, the parent can sit the child on the floor for a few moments and repeat firmly, "Don't touch—just look."

Under ideal conditions, there are several questions that parents can ask themselves before exercising any disciplinary option: How important is this rule? Do I want to confront my child over this particular rule? Can I discipline my child without getting caught up in proving that I am in control?

Although it is important for parents to set consistent limits, it is a matter of record that toddlers accept some rules more slowly than others. It is also a matter of record that toddlers act impulsively. Perhaps the situation is one in which the parent can simply remind the child of the rule and wait a little longer for the child to come around. If, on the other hand, the parent decides that it is time to impose some unpleasant consequence on the child, communication of the idea that the issue is one of control should be avoided. This is a subtle matter, but the choice of words and tone of voice can communicate that there are good reasons for following a rule. Phrases like "I want you to," or "I told you to," especially when spoken in an angry voice, lead children to see the conflict as a battle of wills. Simply saying, "That china vase must not be touched," works better.

\*        \*        \*

The rules about handling objects and the strategies adopted to enforce them reflect both individual parental philosophy and the personality of the child. During the course of the second year, these strategies and rules naturally change as children become more skillful explorers. In this chapter, we have discussed some common strategies for teaching rules about touching: setting limits by location, providing substitute objects, and using verbal prompts. In the long run, the most effective strategy is to help toddlers learn safe ways to touch and carry objects.

Once toddlers have learned some rules about touching, their explorations can be seen in a more positive light. As children poke and prod, pick up and examine, carry and transfer, they are learning about the properties of objects. Differences in size, weight, texture, and durability are being discovered. Although we may not think about it when we mend a piece of broken china, the explorations of the toddler provide basic insights that are essential for future learning.

# Suggested Activities

## Making Things Happen

This popular pop-up toy is a good manipulative toy for one-year olds. It takes a while for children to learn how the five doors are opened, but all of the necessary hand motions are within the capability of one-year olds. When buying a manipulative toy for your child, check how much dexterity and strength are required to operate the toy. Remember that your child will be easily frustrated if he cannot imitate you when you demonstrate with the toy.

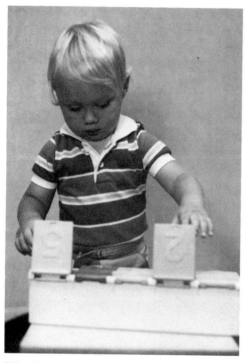 

Wind-up toys represent an exciting category of toys for one year old exploration. However, they vary greatly in the ease with which they are wound and, by this time, your child will want to do the job by himself. Be sure to select toys with large keys (or knobs) that turn easily.

The latches that fascinate one-year olds as they explore cupboards, closets, and window frames can be duplicated on a latch board. If the latches are hinged in some way when they are attached to the board, the manipulative play is even more fun. After all, when something is unlatched it should swing open.

You can create a basket of odds and ends where your child is really free to get her hands on everything. The hardware store, or a hardware junk drawer, is a good place to look for these materials: things with a peculiar shape or feel, objects that come apart and go together, objects that look like they serve a very useful purpose,but you are not sure what it is.

Most one-year olds discover the joy of turning a light switch on and off. Sometimes it takes parents longer to discover that they do not need to stand and hold the child up to the switch. Get a chair, put it next to a wall switch, and let your child stand on it. Then he can touch this amazing object to his heart's content. The switch will not wear out and, when the child begins to wear down, there may be another switch, which activates a different light, that can be explored.

Toddlers can be taught how to handle electrical objects that normally are reserved for adults. Under the direction of an adult, they can turn on the stereo, the television, or the dishwasher. There will be a tendency, of course, for the children to exercise this option over and over again. For a few weeks, parents may need to impress upon their one-year olds that these switches are turned on and off only for a definite purpose. Soon, however, the children will distinguish between "common" switches that can be played with repetitively, like wall switches, and special switches that control expensive equipment.

Toddlers enjoy trying to turn a flashlight on and off, and they are curious about the way the beam of light touches other objects. You can encourage your child to start with flashlight experiments in a well lit room and then progress gradually to dimmer surroundings. A lively light in a dark room can become a very mysterious phenomenon.

A portable radio is another good electrical toy. The knobs represent an interesting problem to be solved. One knob changes the volume, while the other changes the quality of the sound.

Sometimes you can find electrical appliances around the house that are relatively safe. A toddler is not likely to get shocked or burned by an electric

make-up mirror, for example. The child can experiment with different lighting combinations and observe the effect on his own face. It still is a good idea for Mom or Dad to stay nearby and supervise the activity. Probably they will be unable to resist looking in the mirror themselves and making a face.

# Handling Pictures

Babies can be introduced to picture books before they are one year old. Start with a book that has heavy cardboard pages so you won't worry when your baby sucks and chews on them. As soon as your toddler learns how to turn pages properly, give him a chance to look at regular picture books. Many parents report that one-year olds enjoy "reading" by themselves.

One-year olds are attracted to reading materials that they see adults handle. Many of these magazines and catalogs have thin pages that tear accidentally when children play with them. Give your child old copies that you already have read and then count on some damage. If your one-year old starts tearing the pages intentionally, put the magazine or catalog up for a while and substitute a paper product that can be torn, such as old newspapers.

Interesting pictures arrive at your home every day in the junk mail. Let your child help open these envelopes. The mail also brings greeting cards, which are durable pictures, just the right size for one-year olds to handle and carry around.

Photographs of family members are intriguing to one-year olds but often must be handled with care. Try giving your child a few photographs that he can explore on his own. Slip pictures inside a clear plastic cube or a key ring. Or you can make a refrigerator toy by laminating a photograph and mounting a magnetic strip on the back. Still another possibility is to put several pictures in a pocket size photo album and tape the sides of the pages so that the photographs cannot be removed.

# Gentle Touching of Valuable Objects

One of the best ways to teach one-year olds the act of gentle touching is to lift them up to high objects. You give your child a chance to touch something that otherwise would be out of reach and, at the same time, you control the situation. "Just touch," you may say as you lift the child upward. If the child grabs for the object or seems about to act wildly, you simply bring the child back down. By moving the child closer to the object when she touches it gently and moving her farther away when she does not, appropriate behavior will quickly be shaped.

A music box works well for demonstrating why delicate objects are treated

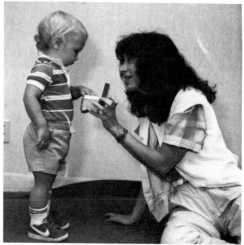

with extra respect. Although a one-year old may not be allowed to pick up the music box, the child can be taught to turn it on and off. Your child can see that gently pulling out the peg or carefully opening the lid starts the sound. Gentle handling is rewarded with a delightful combination of sound and movement, and you can reinforce this lesson with your comments.

Even if you have removed breakable figurines from the ground level of your home, your toddler will find these objects somewhere—on the shelf of a store, or on the coffee table at the home of a relative. You may wish to teach your child how to hold a valuable object for a few seconds and then put it down. In effect, you are introducing a subtle rule: delicate objects sometimes can be handled but only in a brief and tentative manner.

Like busy bees, one-year olds are drawn to the bright colors of flowers, and as the flowers turn to fruits and vegetables, the urge to handle them is over-powering. Sometimes parents can help their children harvest ripe fruits and vegetables; other times the children can be allowed to pick a crop that is going to waste anyway. Much of the time the desire of toddlers to pick flow-

ers, fruits, or vegetables is a source of conflict. Parents can alleviate this conflict by showing their children how to feel these natural wonders with the tips of their fingers. The delicate velvety petal, or the rough texture of a cucumber skin, is quite a surprise in itself and, for children who have just recently entered this world, it may satisfy their curiosity.

# Chapter 2
# EMPTYING AND FILLING

The Scene:   Aunt Minna is visiting her nephew, Karl, age sixteen months.

Aunt Minna:   "Karl, let's put your toys back in the toy basket. Your room looks like a cyclone—Aunt Minna will help."

Karl:   "Minna!"

Aunt Minna:   "Yes, I'm Aunt Minna. You know my name. Now, let's start with your stuffed animals. Come on, Teddy, into the basket you go."

FIVE MINUTES LATER:

Aunt Minna:   "All clean. You're such a big help!"

Karl:   "All clean." (At this point Karl picks up the basket and dumps the toys back on the floor.)

Although emptying and filling are two sides of the same coin, it is emptying, not filling, that most appeals to one year old children. If they have not already discovered the excitement of emptying by their first birthday, they soon will. And for the next few months, emptying behaviors of all kinds will appear. Bookshelves may be cleared, wastebaskets upended, toy boxes emptied. The rule seems to be: find a container, any container, and dump it.

It is logical to dump a container in order to see what is inside or to find a lost toy. Often, however, the toddler has a different goal in mind. Dumping is something to do for the fun of it. Emptying an ashtray, overturning the dog dish, spilling a box of blueberries onto the floor, this is the one-year old's definition of having a good time.

Why are one-year olds so entranced with emptying? A possible explanation is that emptying produces dramatic transformations. A composite object like a bookshelf comes apart into many different pieces when the books are removed. The contents of a wastebasket assume a different shape when they are scattered on the floor. The relationship between container and contained, and the variety of possible transformations, are familiar matters to us as adults. But to one-year olds, these changes are a source of wonderment and a reason for investigation.

Actually, emptying is just the most noticeable transformation that one-year olds investigate. Toddlers also like to move objects from one location to another, perhaps amassing a collection in an unusual spot—under the couch, behind the bookshelf, or in the dirty clothes hamper. Sometimes they intentionally experiment with rearrangements, piling several objects on top of each other or lining them up in a row. Most often, they simply misplace objects by carrying them around for a while and then setting them down somewhere else.

# Setting Limits to Exploration

From a parent's point of view, all this emptying and rearranging behavior on the part of one-year olds tends to have a common consequence. Things around the house are no longer in their customary places and the house looks messy. Parents find themselves seeking ways to limit emptying, even when their housekeeping standards are rather relaxed. An initial step that works for many parents is to alter the physical environment. The parents discourage emptying of wastebaskets by hiding them behind heavy pieces of furniture. They put enticing containers on high shelves or change the location of the dog's dish so that it is less accessible. In general, they reduce the to-

tal number of objects that are within reach of the child. One or two magazines on a table become less tempting than a full magazine rack; a few extra towels in a bathroom linen closet provoke less emptying than a closetful. A shelf or cupboard with a small number of toys can be kept intact more easily than a toy box filled to the brim.

As the children grow older, parents increasingly rely on verbal directives and explanations to limit messy exploration. Gradually, the children learn which emptying activities are unacceptable and which forms will be tolerated to a point. In the process, they also become aware that emptying-is a powerful way to gain attention from adults. For a period of time, emptying can become a cat and mouse game in which the children intentionally violate the rules. They may empty flowerpots by digging out the dirt, or unzip the couch cushions and remove the stuffing that is inside. If parents quickly clean up such messes, the children may be inspired to make an even bigger mess in order to watch their parents work harder.

It is natural for one-year olds and parents to clash over messy exploration. Parents are concerned about maintaining order, while the children are interested in emptying, transferring and rearranging objects. If parents make too much out of this difference, however, they invite a power struggle. Confrontations are best avoided by setting limits to messy exploration while at the same time not over-reacting when children go beyond these limits. Within a few months, parents will see that their children are beginning to adopt the family rules concerning messy exploration.

# Encouraging Constructive Exploration

Teaching and reinforcing workable limits for messy exploration is a reasonable goal. This goal is furthered when parents encourage forms of exploration that promote order. Although many one-year olds are fascinated with emptying, they are also attracted to filling. A twelve month old baby already enjoys dropping stones into a bucket, or stuffing cookies into a cup of juice. Between one and two years of age, this interest in filling grows steadily. Some filling experiments, such as stuffing socks into the toilet, can be just as troublesome as emptying behavior, but filling activities are generally constructive. Instead of taking things apart, the children are putting them together and they often help accomplish a family task at the same time.

Among the constructive filling jobs that toddlers manage at an early age are filling the wastebasket with newspaper, or filling the hamper with laundry. Recognizing that such filling activities carry adult prestige, toddlers carry out these chores with great enthusiasm. Brian, at fourteen months, considered himself custodian of the vegetable bin. After each trip to the grocery store, he painstakingly lined up the onions on the bottom shelf of the bin. Benjamin became quite adept at arranging the canned food on the bottom shelf of the pantry. Many toddlers enjoy putting dishes in the dishwasher, or putting clothes into the dryer.

One-year olds can also be encouraged to pursue a variety of play activities that involve filling. Children generally fill a container in order to empty

it, which means that the activity does not last unless a cycle is set up—filling, then emptying; filling, then emptying; filling, then emptying. This kind of cyclic play occurs easily enough with water and sand. It can also occur with substances such as rice, dried macaroni, or cheerios. The children are so intrigued by the process of pouring that they keep refilling their containers.

In order to establish the same kind of cycle with other play materials, there needs to be some special incentive for filling. Most often the factor that pro-

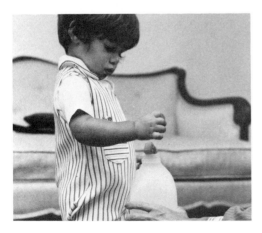 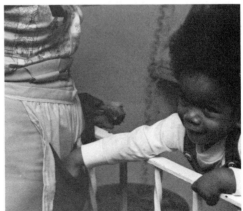

vides this extra incentive is an unusual container. An empty gallon milk jug is fun to fill with small objects, such as raisins or cheerios. Leftover shopping bags, or old purses that are easy to open, stimulate filling. Pockets of any kind on the clothes of one-year olds are fascinating containers.

The attraction of filling becomes still greater when children become interested in transferring material from one container to another. In their water play, for example, older toddlers try to pour water from one cup to another. Once parents sense that their children are interested in the transfer idea, a

 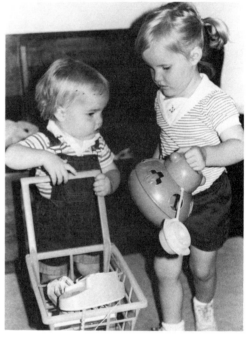

second container can be introduced into a familiar routine.

If a child enjoys emptying a junk drawer in the kitchen, the parent might show him how to fill a toy shopping cart (or a shopping bag) with things from the drawer, as if they were on a shopping trip. Later, the child could be encouraged to transfer the items back to the junk drawer. If children enjoy putting objects like rocks or walnuts into a plastic bowl, add a second bowl with water in it. Transferring, from the wet to the dry and vice versa, can be demonstrated and parents can then wait to see if the idea catches on. Muffin tins and egg cartons are particularly versatile. A handful of raisins or cheerios can be distributed again and again until they end up in someone's stomach.

The most advanced form of filling for one-year olds is puzzle play. Puzzles represent a category of containers in which the contents must be arranged in a precise manner. During the latter half of the second year, many children are able to complete very simple inset puzzles, although they often need help orienting the puzzle pieces properly. The children know where a piece belongs, but they do not know how to rotate the piece until it is perfectly in line with the hole.

When parents help one-year olds finish an inset puzzle, or fit plastic shapes into a shape sorter, the children experience an intense feeling of accomplishment. They begin to see the satisfaction of filling. At the same time, however, this kind of precision filling is potentially very frustrating. In fact, few things distress one-year olds more than a puzzle that does not behave according to expectations.

Rather than frustrate children with inset puzzles before they are ready, some parents create their own puzzles out of simple containers. A hole big enough for a small block to pass through can be cut in the lid of a coffee can, or a hole big enough for crayons can be cut in the top of a potato chip can. Containers like these are size sorters, easier to master than the shape sorters sold in toy stores. One-year olds do not have to fill each hole with a particular shape, but they do have to pay attention to size attributes.

Included in this intermediate territory of beginning puzzles is the case of the round peg in a round hole. Putting a round peg in a round hole offers one-year olds the satisfaction of an inset puzzle without the accompanying frustration. Like an inset puzzle, the fit is precise, but there is no orientation problem. Large scale pegboards, in which the pegs can be grasped readily, are traditional favorites. Another popular version of round pegs in round holes has appeared in recent years: miniature dolls that can be placed in furniture, cars and other vehicles.

In reality, there are many intermediate points between the elementary task of filling a bucket with rocks and the demanding task of completing an inset puzzle. A whole range of containers are possible and, with each one, children learn something about shape and size. A narrow-necked bottle cannot be filled with large objects, an envelope will not accommodate objects that are too thick, and objects that are too long will stick out of a pocket. As children take into account the peculiarities of different containers, they are beginning to understand the nature of puzzles.

# Individual Differences

When one-year olds are playing with a pegboard, or with miniature dolls, one of their favorite activities is to stick their fingers in the holes. Filling this space with their fingers is one way to learn about spatial relationships. At the other extreme, some one-year olds investigate spatial relationships by filling spaces with their whole bodies. They crawl into cupboards or giant boxes, climb into the clothes hamper, or squeeze between the wall and the bed frame.

The way one-year olds use their own bodies to fill containers may reflect a certain style of manipulative play. Although all children handle and rearrange objects with their fingers, some children seem particularly fascinated with small scale exploration. Other children seem drawn to emptying and filling on a large scale. A child who thinks small will be attracted to different activities than a child who things big.

The "think small" child may be especially interested in squeezing the toothpaste out of the tube, fitting playing cards into a narrow box, or in-

serting keys into keyholes. The "think big" child is more likely to empty the bottom two shelves of the pantry or fill the hamper with a variety of clothes and toys. Parents can help their children develop constructive filling activities by keeping in mind these individual differences. If the child enjoys playing with big things, the parent might buy a set of large nesting blocks, or a wagon for carting stones around the yard. If the child is interested in small things, parents may try miniature "people" that fit into vehicles, a wallet with paper "money," or an inset puzzle with knobs.

\*      \*      \*

In this chapter we have discussed a major form of manipulative play among one year old children—emptying and filling. Parents see the emptying first, and quite possibly they see too much of it. Their immediate reaction is to wonder how this emptying can be controlled. Most parents set limits that define certain messy forms of exploration as unacceptable. A more positive approach is to encourage constructive forms of exploration, especially filling. Encouraging one-year olds to fill containers not only reduces emptying but also promotes the development of new skills.

For a long time, of course, emptying has the upper hand. Even after a period of play filling, or after a period of thoughtful rearranging, one-year olds usually leave the materials in a cluttered state. There is a big difference, however, between an older toddler who leaves a mess after an extended play period and one who simply dumps a container and then walks away. Children who are learning to organize and fill, as well as to empty, are learning how to translate their curiosity about objects into sustained play.

# Suggested Activities

## *Toys for Filling*

Toddlers enjoy filling shape sorters, but if there are many different shapes, they probably will need a helping hand from Mom or Dad. Much simpler is a home-made sorting toy with only one hole through which your child can stuff a variety of objects. In this case, your job will be to take the lid off periodically and remove the contents so that your child can start all over again.

A pegboard with large pegs stimulates a simple filling activity. Stacking toys serve the same purpose. You can make a home-made stacking toy with plastic lids and a spindle.

Older toddlers may be able to fill single piece puzzles. Younger toddlers have more fun with home-made puzzles, such as a box and paper towel roll.

Cannisters that have been used in child care, like this baby-wipe container, hold special appeal for one-year olds. When they are empty, give your child those plastic bottles and jars he has been trying to reach on the changing table or in the bathroom.

A gallon milk jug is an interesting container for filling because the narrow neck is such a contrast to the spacious interior. Put some raisins inside a jug and let your one-year old figure out how to pour them out. For a more advanced filling activity, encourage your child to fit a long necklace inside the jug.

Your one-year old probably likes containers with screw-on lids, although she may need help getting the lid on and off. Once the lid is off, she will be receptive to the idea of putting something inside before closing up the container.

Ziploc bags are another one of those "important" containers that toddlers see adults using. Somewhat like envelopes, they open and close in an unusual way, which makes the prospect of filling them more inviting. Try putting some miniature dolls, or other small treasures, in a Ziploc bag and see how your child responds.

Your one-year old likes to investigate purses. Unfortunately, from the child's viewpoint, many purses are hard to open. Give your child one that stays open, like a shopping bag, and encourage her to fill it. A purse can be filled with traditional items, such as a hairbrush or an old wallet, or with unorthodox things such as balls, books, and trucks. A long strap, which allows your child to carry the purse over her shoulder, will further increase its appeal.

One-year olds are learning about presents, those containers that are brightly decorated and arrive on holidays. You can create everyday presents for your child as well. One way is to wrap a favorite toy in a piece of aluminum foil, put it on your child's plate at lunch or in his crib at naptime, and encourage him to unwrap it. Another way is to make a "surprise box" by using a box with a lift-off lid, like a shoebox. The lid and sides of the box can be covered with stickers and ribbons, while you can put inside something of interest to your child.

# Filling Activities

Filling is a natural activity in a sandbox because, the larger the container that you fill, the more fun you get pouring the sand out. Try giving your one-year old a spoon or scoop to use as a tool for filling. Many children at this age are trying to learn how to use a spoon and fork at the table. Spooning up sand provides a good practice exercise, for spills are of no consequence.

 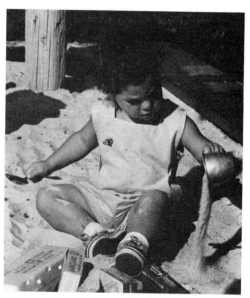

Another natural filling activity is to put things in a pocket. Because many clothes for toddlers do not have pockets, the children treat these accessories as luxuries. You might consider making a smock or an apron with pockets for your child. "What's in your pocket today?" is a good conversation starter with a one-year old who is lucky enough to have a pocket to fill.

A perennial favorite at all ages is filling a container with water from a hose. One-year olds may be instructed to fill outdoor flower pots with the correct amount of water, or they may try filling different sizes of tin cans and buckets. On occasion, they may fill a wading pool. The simplest approach is to show a one-year old how to fill the depression at the base of a tree or shrub. Rarely can these plants be overwatered, and in a short while the water sinks into the ground revealing once again a hole to be filled.

When taking a walk, carry along a pail. Small objects that interest you and your one-year old can be dropped inside. Soon your child will get the idea and start making his own contributions. He may even take over the job of carrying the container. Don't be surprised if he wants to dump the contents from time to time and begin again with a clean pail. Collected items are not necessarily meant to be kept at this age.

Filling a book makes sense to toddlers, as long as they can empty it at the same time. Photograph albums and scrapbooks, however, cannot take this kind of continuous reconstruction. You can create a satisfactory substitute with a blank photo album and a set of colorform characters. The colorforms, which are thin plastic shapes, will stick to the plastic coated pages of the album. Your child can move them from page to page endlessly, with no damage to either the album or the colorforms. If you want to give the pages more of a storybook look, put magazine pictures on the sticky surface inside the plastic covers. Then your child can place the colorforms in different settings: a living room, a car, a mountain scene, and so on.

Fisher-Price characters, and similar miniature dolls, are often sold with extensive playscapes: an airport, a castle, or a dollhouse. One-year olds, however, are more interested in individual accessories for the "little people," especially accessories that have a hole for holding a little person's bottom. If your one-year old likes to handle these little dolls, try to buy accessories like cars, buses, chairs and toilets. Then your child will be able to fill and refill the holes with her new found friends.

The kitchen offers many opportunities for filling activities. One that does not task the skills of a toddler is putting food away. With your help, a one-year old may learn to remove specific items from the table everyday and put them in the cupboard or the refrigerator. Even more exciting is stocking the kitchen after grocery shopping. Toddlers can put canned goods or cereal boxes in low cupboards, fill a crisper with vegetables that do not bruise easily, or arrange cheese and cold cuts in the proper compartment of the refrigerator.

Rather than storing your child's toys in a single toy box or laundry basket, keep them in several smaller baskets. The toys will be easier to find and your child will be stimulated to transfer items from one basket to another.

Small pieces of food, like Cheerios or raisins, are especially good for filling games that involve transferring. Place two or more containers on a table, put the food in one of them, and show your child the idea of redistributing the food among the containers. A little here, a little there, and a little in your mouth.

Water is a superior medium for transfer play. The dribbles and spills are managed by setting up the activity outside. A variety of spoons, measuring cups and metal bowls serve as non-breakable containers, and they make pleasant clinking sounds as the child plays. Try adding ice cubes to the water. They bob and float in the water, slither around in a child's hand or mouth, make a splash when poured, and eventually disappear altogether!

 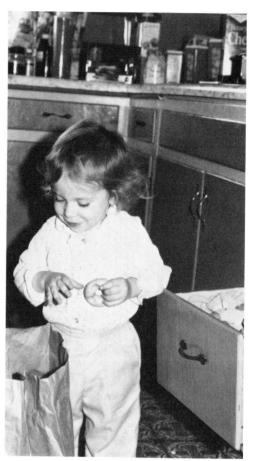

Your toddler probably has a drawer or cupboard in the kitchen for exploration. Typically this place is emptied out day after day until, eventually, the child grows bored. You can stimulate filling and rekindle interest in this junk drawer by introducing imaginary shopping. Armed with a shopping bag (or your child's toy shopping cart), accompany your child to the drawer and pretend to purchase some of the items. Later in the day, they can be dumped back in the drawer. If your child likes this way of playing, stock the drawer with objects that fit her shopping interests.

## For Those Who Think Big

A large, plastic garbage can is an ideal toy for children who favor oversize containers. Even if they can barely see over the top of the can, they will find a way to fill it with every imaginable sort of "garbage."

Children who think big like to get inside containers themselves. In fact, a large box may become a second home. Parents can extend this play by delivering things to the new address. "Knock, knock—here's some mail for you," a parent might announce as he hands in a book or a stuffed animal. In all likelihood, the child will respond by later carrying additional posessions to the new quarters.

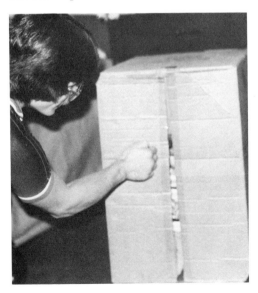
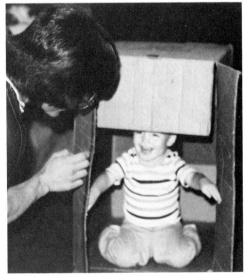

Putting trash in a wastebasket or garbage sack is fun for most toddlers. Children who want to go one step further can be encouraged to take a full receptacle to the outside garbage can and dump it in. Some trash may fall on the ground and probably the child will need help with the garbage can lid, but for a child who thinks big, this is a filling activity that is most gratifying.

# Chapter 3
# NEW MUSCLE POWER

| | |
|---|---|
| The Scene: | Two mothers with their children at a park. |
| First-time Mother: | "Look at that—Your Jeffrey—He's standing up by himself! He's going to be walking any day now." |
| Jeff's Mother: | "Yes, I suppose you're right." |
| First-time Mother: | "Look, look at Jeff—he did it! He's walking by himself. He took four steps!" |
| Jeff's Mother: | "It's exciting, isn't it? But now it means he's going to be harder to keep track of." |

Experienced parents like Jeff's mother recognize that a child's first steps may be a mixed blessing. The excitement of seeing their baby develop such an important skill is tempered by the knowledge that walking ushers in a new era, one in which the baby will require greater supervision.

Whether they are early or late walkers, most children become accomplished walkers between the ages of one and two. Some children burst into walking, while others inch their way. Children who are on the heavy side, who are temperamentally cautious, or who are focusing their energies on other developmental tasks are likely to be slow walkers. The normal limits for walking, however, are broad and extend from eight to twenty months. As long as a youngster is within this normal range, the age at which walking begins tells us little about other facets of the child's intelligence.

Quite literally, walking brings with it a new worldview. Growing a foot taller overnight makes the world look different, and getting around is different as well. Familiar patterns of movement must be relearned to mesh with walking. Turning around, sitting down, going under and over obstacles, all are changed when undertaken from a standing rather than a crawling position.

Parents often note that when one-year olds gain control of walking, they look so much older. The act of walking does seem to give a child a sense of being grown-up, and with this sense comes an infusion of self confidence and vigor. There is a strong need to take on new challenges and discover new capabilities. In their excitement, the children test themselves to the limit, struggling and straining to accomplish feats they see older people performing.

Frequently, one-year olds undertake more than they can manage and are frustrated. Why, parents may wonder, does my child always have to do things the hard way? Why does he have to push the baby carriage through that narrow doorway? Why is he still climbing on the bed after just falling off? Like climbing a mountain because it is there, taking on new obstacles is a means of self-definition for the one-year old. "The more powerful I am phys-

ically," the child seems to be thinking." the more significant I am as a person."

# Lifting and Carrying

In the initial stages, walking is a matter of using hands as well as feet. Babies pull themselves to a standing position, and hold on to pieces of furniture in order to sidestep around a room. Even when babies no longer need to hold onto things for support, they often hold something in their hands as a source of security.

As children become more adept at walking with their hands full, they challenge themselves to carry larger and heavier loads. A purse is replaced by a heavy briefcase, or a small rubber ball by a big basketball. Typically, parents respond to such achievements with words of praise. "Oh, you are a strong boy lifting that great big basketball!" "What a big girl to carry Daddy's briefcase!" Because they are proud of their one-year old's new lifting ability, parents reinforce the connection between being grown-up and being physically powerful.

# Pushing and Pulling

There are other ways for one-year olds to keep their hands busy when walking. Objects can be pushed or pulled. Pushing actually facilitates walking because children can lean on the pushed object and, with practice, they learn to look ahead and steer while they are pushing. Pulling, by contrast, is more difficult. Children need to look back and forth as they pull, now ahead to see what is coming, now behind to see how the pulled object is progressing. When they first discover pull toys, toddlers are likely to go around the house searching for other objects to pull. However, once each pull toy is mastered, it tends to lose its appeal. The future lies with pushing, steering, and ultimately pretending to drive.

One of the most popular push toys is a popper, a kind of walking stick that makes music or creates an interesting visual display when it is pushed. One-year olds can achieve the same type of effect, but with less fanfare, by pushing a broom, a mop, or even a tennis racket around the house. Alexis, at fourteen months, discovered an old guitar and came thumping down the hall, pushing it along like a hockey stick. What these household items lack in the way of fancy colors and unusual noises, they make up for in status by being adult objects.

Toys with wheels are even better for pushing. Toddlers continue to push miniature vehicles on their hands and knees, but they also discover that walking gives them enough leverage to push larger vehicles. Grunting and

groaning, the children are capable of maneuvering a surprising assortment of such objects: strollers, grocery carts, tricycles and wheelbarrows. Unfortunately, these vehicles often get stuck in a tight spot or crash into some obstacle.

Parents can avoid some problems by encouraging their children to become interested in smaller versions of these vehicles. A toy shopping cart is more manageable than a grocery cart, a doll buggy (or doll stroller) is better than a regular stroller, a push-type riding toy is more satisfactory than a tricycle. These push toys are a good investment and, if possible, parents should buy both a riding toy and a cart/buggy toy. Within a short time they will be used differently, the one for pretend driving and the other for pretend shopping and doll play.

As a one-year old tries out a variety of pushing feats, problems sometimes arise. Adam, at one year, had an absolute fetish about shutting doors. Despite his mother's fears, he was quite adept at keeping his fingers from getting pinched. However, Adam's door shutting mania still created problems because, as soon as a door was shut, he wanted it open again. Finally, Adam's mother draped towels over the top of Adam's favorite doors so that they would not shut completely when he pushed them.

Eventually Adam got bored with pushing doors and devoted his energies to pushing furniture around. This was no problem until he discovered that a chair could be pushed up to a counter and used as a stepladder to get onto the counter. The solution this time, Adam's parents decided, was to teach him how to stand on the chair and help with counter work.

Despite the occasional problems that occur, the pushing and pulling skills of one-year olds find acceptable outlets. There are enough opportunities to practice without becoming destructive or endangering anyone. As was the case with lifting, parents and children are able to agree that this new form of muscle power is a sign of maturity.

# Throwing, Pounding, and Climbing

Not all forms of one-year old muscle power are so easily accommodated to everyday life. Between the ages of one and two, children learn to swing their arms forcefully and to direct the impact of this swinging motion in a particular direction at a particular spot. In plain words, they discover how to throw and to pound. Throwing and pounding can be very destructive behavior unless performed with accuracy and selectivity. One-year olds who are just testing their new abilities are neither accurate nor selective. Any object is fair game in their opinion and, if it makes a splat, a thud, or some other interesting sound, so much the better. One-year olds may not be bent on destruction when they throw and pound but they are not very upset by it either.

When one-year olds enthusiastically whack a dinner plate with a spoon, or toss food on the floor, parents clearly recognize the gulf that separates them from their children. From the child's point of view, throwing and pounding is a glorious display of power. From the parent's perspective, however, this throwing and pounding looks like destructive behavior that needs to be restricted.

The most common strategy for coping with pounding and throwing is re-direction. The child who is pounding on a dinner plate can be redirected to a pounding bench or an xylophone. The child who is throwing food can be taken out of the high chair and given a ball to throw. Verbal prompts like

"Balls are for throwing" may help with a child who is tuned into language. However, as opportunities to practice throwing and pounding are restricted, the children lose some of their feelings of exhilaration. Their feelings of ac-complishment, which accompany any new physical skill, have been dimin-ished.

Much the same process occurs with another form of new muscle power—climbing. At first climbing is primarily a means of getting onto adult pieces of furniture. Toddlers learn to climb onto adult-sized chairs, beds and sofas. Most parents are pleased that their children are learning a new skill and encourage them to sit down when they reach the top. In time, however, one-year olds climb higher and parents withdraw much of their support. Par-ents get increasingly upset as their children practice climbing on the kitchen counter, the dining table, or the bedroom dressers.

In actuality, it would be misleading to exaggerate the conflicts over throwing, pounding and climbing that take place between parents and one-year olds. Families do find ways for one-year olds to experiment with these new skills. In many homes, for example, various throwing games arise. A diaper may be tossed back and forth as part of a dressing routine, or dirty clothes may be thrown in the hamper. Rag dolls and stuffed animals have a tendency to leap from one family member to another.

Pounding, which has been directed toward a cobbler's bench or xylophone, can be extended to other objects if parents are free to supervise. Obviously, the blows of a one-year old cannot harm such things as a carpet, or the cushions on a couch. If the children use a small rubber hammer, they can tap on floors, walls, non-breakable toys and appliances without causing any real damage.

Greater climbing also can be allowed with parental supervision. Younger toddlers can be permitted to climb up and down stairs, while older toddlers

can practice climbing on a sturdy changing table, or perhaps into the crib. Under the watchful eye of parents, the children can be allowed to climb up to counters on specific occasions, such as climbing on the bathroom counter when it is time to brush their teeth. Climbing to a higher spot may be acceptable when the purpose is to watch something rather than to get into mischief. A one-year old might stand on a chair to watch Mommy making a cake, to find the fish in the aquarium, or to look at the cars out the window.

Throwing, pounding and climbing are far from forbidden activities in most homes. However, the fact remains that these new forms of muscle power are seldom exercised freely. Throwing soft materials, or pounding with a toy hammer, is better than no throwing or pounding, yet it is not quite the real thing. Feelings of mastery and potency are somewhat muted. Moreover, the limited number of opportunities to throw, pound, or climb means that the rules for such exploration are complicated. How soft does something have to be before it can be thrown? How hard can something be hit without causing damage? How high is too high when climbing on the furniture?

# Finding a New Environment

There is no simple way out of this quandary, but parents can look for a play environment in which throwing, pounding and climbing are more welcome. Most parents discover that the best play environment for a physically active toddler is outdoors. Outside the house there are fewer valuables to break by throwing or pounding, and fewer off-limit areas to reach by climbing. Although climbing, throwing and pounding remain potentially destructive and always require supervision, children can be given greater leeway outdoors to test themselves against the world of objects.

A variety of outdoor environments is available for exercising new muscle power. Water can be splashed in a wading pool, and dirt can be pounded with the back of a shovel. A toddler can tap on the garbage can, the backyard fence, or an old tree stump. Balls can be bounced in a driveway or thrown against the side of a garage. A small hill in the backyard makes a fine back board for a large rubber ball. When the child throws the ball up the hill, it comes back by itself. There are moderate, and reasonably safe, climbing opportunities—a picnic table, a pile of sand, the steps of a slide. Parks and other outdoor spaces can be explored. Simply walking around the block will bring out new opportunities for physical feats.

Gym environments, when they are available, are also excellent for one-year old muscle power. Toddlers can climb on apparatus designed for short legs, and can try out all sorts of walking, balancing, sliding and jumping skills. They can throw balls with gusto. They can push and pull. In some toddler gyms, even pounding opportunities are provided. The growing popularity of these gyms reflects our increased recognition that one-year olds have the need and the right to practice all of their physical skills.

\*       \*       \*

This chapter has looked at the ways young children explore and expand their muscle power. As with other aspects of exploration, parents seek a balance between setting limits and allowing children free rein. In reaching this balance point, power struggles can take place, especially during the first flush of a new physical skill.

An effective way for parents to diffuse these power struggles is to find an acceptable way for children to practice a new skill. Children who insist on throwing, for example, may be given a set of beanbags and encouraged to throw them at appropriate targets. Children who insist on climbing may be

given a safe place where they can climb up and jump down. By providing safe ways for children to practice emerging skills, and by encouraging children to "perform" in these safe places, conflicts are reduced to a minimum.

Sometimes a child's opportunities to practice new physical skills are, by necessity, restricted in a home environment. In these situations, children will gain a stronger sense of physical prowess if other environments are provided. A fenced-in backyard, a porch, a garage, a neighborhood park, or a toddler gym are possible arenas for vigorous play. As a parent, you will see that your child's new muscle power means a new sense of self. By encouraging physical development, you can support that sense of self and help your child preserve the feelings of joy that accompany each new achievement.

# Suggested Activities

## *Pushing, Pulling, and Lifting*

The primary appeal of pull toys is their novelty. You can create a supply of new pull toys simply by attaching different objects to a rope. A parent can use empty lemon juice containers for a pull toy. Try making a pull train out of boxes, egg cartons, gallon milk jugs, or tin cans.

Your one-year old cannot operate a full-size broom or mop with any efficiency. Nevertheless, he may get a thrill from pushing and pulling such a long stick. Find a space big enough for safe maneuvers and give your child a chance to experiment with toys like these.

A modified version of tetherball may appeal to your child's pushing instincts. String up a ball with plastic holders from six-packs and let him get started. An older one-year old may enjoy hitting the suspended ball with a short handled mallet or paddle.

Sooner or later, one-year olds seem to try pushing furniture around the house. Not only is much of it too heavy but it is also not made to be pushed. A sofa bolster is an exception to the rule. It is light, rolls easily when pushed, and hurts nothing. Encourage a one-year old who is challenging the furniture to lug and push a sofa bolster. If one is not available, try substituting a sleeping bag or a beach ball.

Of course, one of the favorite push toys of children is a toy car or truck. Small vehicles tend to be driven over pieces of furniture. A dining table provides a particularly fine play arena. The cars and trucks roll easily across the surface and form interesting configurations as they are positioned or parked on the table.

Pushing is allied with steering. Pushing and steering a large wheel toy represents an exciting challenge for one-year olds. Whether they sit on the toy and push with their feet or walk behind and push, you will see them mastering this challenge step by step, learning to reverse directions when they run into a wall, to negotiate tight turns and narrow doorways, to retrace a path or complete a circular route. These toys come in many forms, and one-year olds seem to enjoy all of them. If possible, provide your child with both a riding toy and a cart-type toy, since they involve different movements and lead to different kinds of imaginary play.

The sense of power that drives one-year olds to push and pull large objects also compels them to try lifting and carrying heavy loads. These weight-lifting experiments are most successful when an object looks heavier than it really is. Lifting an empty briefcase or hoisting a large inflatable toy gives an obvious boost to your one-year old's feelings of pride and accomplishment.

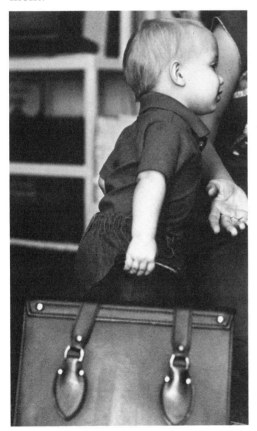
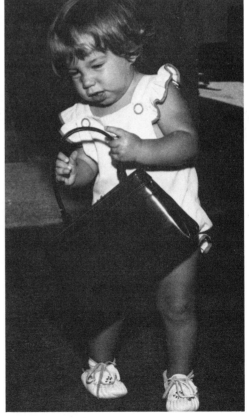

## Climbing

If you have a young toddler who wants to climb, put pillows or bean bag chairs in the corner of a room. This will give her a safe experience.

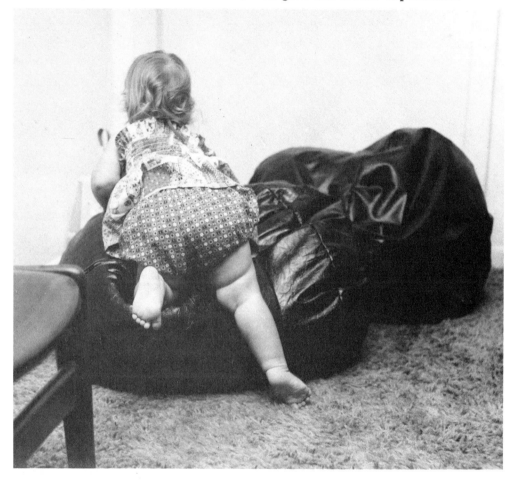

Many one-year olds like to climb up on furniture and then stand on it. Parents typically discourage this behavior. An exception that makes sense is letting your child stand on furniture in order to look out the window. Even a young toddler can balance herself on a sofa and look out the living room window at passing motorists, school children, and neighborhood dogs. An older toddler is coordinated enough to stand on a chair and look out other windows in the house. Being able to see what is going on in the outside world adds a new dimension to your child's daily routine and may occupy a considerable period of time.

You may wish to give your child a lightweight stool to carry around. This piece of portable, child-size furniture adds greatly to the child's sense of freedom. Be sure the stool is safe to stand on. A hassock filled with foam rubber is particularly good because it is both stable and light. Even if the new piece of furniture elevates your child only a few inches off the ground, it gives him insight into the principle of stepping stones. Your child may see new footholds in the furniture, and ascend to new heights.

Another reason for climbing on furniture is to be able to jump back down. Perhaps you and your child can find a place in the house for this climbing and jumping. One possibility is to remove a cushion from the couch. The child can use this shallow pit, which is nearer to the floor, as a jumping platform and, because the cushion has been removed, the couch is subject to less abuse. With a young toddler you may want to build up the landing spot with a pillow, for a fall of a few inches is tantalizing enough. As the child grows older, he will look for drop-offs of one to two feet.

As soon as they are able, children try to climb on beds. Water beds seem to be even more popular with one-year olds than traditional beds. They tend to be lower, which makes them easier to climb on, and they respond to the movements of the child. Regardless of the type of bed, parents worry that their one-year olds will fall and hurt themselves on the frame or the floor. Some parents manage this problem by closely watching their children and teaching them to play in the middle of the bed. Others establish a routine of playing with the children. Although some accidents still occur, most toddlers and their parents find that a bed, and especially a water bed, is an irresistable climbing toy.

Some one-year olds like to climb on the couch and then walk back and forth, treating the couch like a bridge or a ledge. You can create this kind of climbing opportunity by using a wide board as a balance beam. The board can be raised higher as a child becomes more adept. Most of the time, one-year olds are aware of their limitations and will explore a new bridge cautiously, like the girl in this picture. If a new bridge intimidates your child, make the task easier by placing the balance beam next to a wall.

## Throwing

A ping pong ball is ideal for indoor throwing. It can be thrown vigorously without damaging anything. On a hard surface, it bounces and rolls energetically. Even in the bathtub its characteristics will amuse your one-year old.

Bean bags can be made by filling small plastic bags with non-breakable materials, like sand or macaroni. You can use these bean bags to show your one-year old how to throw at a target. The target may be simply an open box on a chair, or you may draw a design on the side of a box and cut out large holes for the bean bags to pass through. Throwing at a safe target keeps indoor throwing within manageable limits.

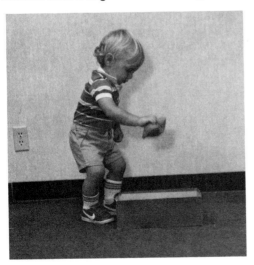

If your one-year old continues to throw too many things indoors, you may want to work harder at transferring this behavior to an outdoor setting. Few activities have greater appeal than throwing objects into water. Put a wading pool in a shady spot and let your child practice throwing whatever small objects are available in abundance—rocks, nuts, pine cones, crabapples. Some mess will result, but your child's penchant for throwing will not cause damage, and both of you will be happier.

# Pounding

A toy workbench is good for letting one-year olds hammer vigorously, but it means that the child's exploration must be restricted to one spot. You may also want to purchase a miniature tool set. Whether made of plastic, hard rubber, or even metal, these tiny tools are not big enough to cause much damage, yet one-year olds see them as comparable to real tools and are satisfied pounding and poking all over the house with them. In fact, as older toddlers begin to pretend to fix things, they actually seem to prefer tools that cannot possibly have any effect. Perhaps it is easier to maintain the illusion that way.

A good environment for experimental tapping and hammering is the garage (when the car is not parked in it.) The walls of a garage are usually unfinished, the floor is cement, and there are wood scraps and junk metal to pound on.

A one-year old can use a flat tool, like a spatula or the back of a shovel, to firm and shape sand. Besides, it is just plain fun to pound on sand. When your toddler is in a hammering mood, let him beat on a sandpile for a while.

## Exercising New Muscle Power at the Park or Gym

Your home is not always well suited to the outbursts of new muscle power from your one-year old. The equipment at a park or gym, on the other hand, has been designed for just this purpose. Give your child regular opportun-

ities to explore these muscle building environments, and when you and your toddler are in conflict at home over a specific form of vigorous exploration, try to find an alternative outlet at the park or the gym.

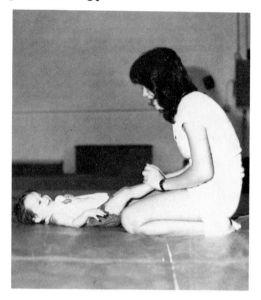

# Chapter 4
# THE TIMID EXPLORER

The Scene:    A public beach on Sunday.

Father:    (Carrying a picnic basket, several beach towels, an overstuffed teddy bear, and a diaper bag.) "It was quite a ride, but it's worth it. This place is gorgeous and Courtney will love playing in the sand!"

Mother:    (Putting Courtney down.) "Feel the sand between your toes. Doesn't it feel good?"

Courtney:    (After standing in the sand for a second.) "Upie, upie. Dadda upie. Go home."

Throughout the first chapters, we have emphasized the role of parents in setting limits and establishing rules. Children, however, are not always enthusiastic about independent exploration. In some situations they are fearful of discomfort or some hidden danger. Unpleasant sensations, such as loud noises, bright lights, or unusual textures may disturb them. The sound of waves pounding on the shore or the flash of a camera may send them into a panic. Parents naturally want their children to conquer what seem to be illogical fears. We need to remember, however, that adult perceptions of "safe" and 'dangerous' are not the same as those of a toddler. Just as parents help their children avoid activities that look safe but really are dangerous, so should they help their children explore situations that may appear dangerous from a toddler's perspective but are really very safe.

The frightening nature of a strange stimulus can sometimes be blotted out by introducing more familiar sensations. Loud fireworks, for example, become less fear-provoking when parents clap loudly and cheer after each explosion. Essentially, this technique involves distracting children, redirecting their attention. A one-year old may stand uncertainly in a wading pool, apparently immobilized by the cold water. Then, when the parent directs the child's attention toward slapping the water and making splashes, the child forgets the unusual feel of the pool and starts exploring.

At other times, parents can help fearful one-year olds with words, not so much by talking them out of their fear but by offering the right labels. Being able to label the fearful or disagreeable element in a situation gives young children a sense of power. The wading pool is "cold," the camera flash is "bright," ocean waves are "loud," sand is "scratchy." The particular words that parents use are not as important as the tone of confidence with which they are spoken. Seeing that a problem can be "captured" with words, one-year olds try to imitate and feel more in control.

Probably the most effective technique of all is to desensitize fearful children. By exposing them to situations that are similar, but not as frightening, one-year olds gradually learn to expand their range of exploration. The child who avoids sand at the beach can be exposed to a sandbox at home; the child who dislikes grass at the park can play on a blanket on the front lawn. A fear of bright light may be alleviated by giving the child a flashlight; a fear of loud noises may be lessened by giving the child a big bell. There are no magic answers, no series of precise steps to be followed in desensitizing a fearful one-year old. Parents must simply try different ideas as they think of them, keeping in mind that it will take time for their children to overcome fears.

Older toddlers may show a different pattern of fearfulness. Suddenly, and unpredictably, they are afraid of unusual creatures—clowns, automated characters, or large animals. There is still a perceptual dimension to this fear, in that the feared objects look and sound different but, beyond that, the children are worried about what these creatures might do. No longer so naive about the world, the children seem to be imagining that the unusual creatures will hurt them. They are losing their innocence and the specter of "monsters" is clearly on the horizon.

Because toddlers sometimes are so funny when they first develop an imaginary fear, opening their eyes like saucers or diving into their parent's lap, parents may be tempted to tease them with the awesome object. Karen

screamed at the sight of a Halloween mask. Her older brother and sister, who knew that the mask was harmless, took turns putting on the mask to watch their sister's reactions. This kind of repeated experience can produce a long lasting fear that may be difficult to modify.

It is better to help children get familiar with scary things in a gradual way. Pamela was petrified when she first encountered Micky Mouse on a trip to Disney World. Back in the motel room, Pam's mother eased her fear by showing her Mickey Mouse's picture in a book and then buying her a miniature mouse. That afternoon Pam was given a chance to pet a larger Mickey Mouse in the toy store. By the end of the trip, Pamela bravely touched "real" Mickey Mouse's hand with the tip of her index finger.

Parents can use a variety of techniques to help children overcome imaginary fears. In addition to gradual exposure, they can let their children watch the frightening object from a safe distance. They can associate a positive word like "pretty" with the scary thing, or they can tell the child to wave "goodbye" as soon as it appears. (Knowing that Gretchen was afraid of beards, Gretchen's mother would say, "There's a man with a beard over there—let's wave goodbye.") These techniques, without forcing one-year olds to interact with frightening people, puppets, or animals, help the children gain a sense of control.

In general, fearfulness is relatively uncommon at this stage. More common is fussiness, a condition hard to describe but easy enough for parents to recognize. Instead of getting into focused, independent exploration, the one-year old is at loose ends, casting about for something to do. Often the child whines and hangs on a parent's leg. In earlier chapters we have suggested activities for just such situations. Naturally, each child will not enjoy all of these activities, but there will be some from each chapter that are appealing.

More importantly, individual children will display preferences for certain types of exploration. By responding to these preferences, parents can counteract fussiness. The child may always be on the lookout for an object with a movable part, something to turn on or to take apart. The child may be a re-arranger, someone who likes to move objects from one location to another, taking them out of one spot and squirreling them away in another. He may be a muscle user who glories in heavy work and vigorous exercise. Add to these distinctions, (which correspond to our chapter topics,) other differences in preferred exploration, such as indoors versus outdoors, toys versus household objects, private versus social play, and parents will begin to discern and foster their child's unique style of exploration.

One-year olds really are different from each other, and each child may have an extraordinary interest in a specific mode of exploration. Although most one-year olds show little interest in independent block building, a few children will diligently stack blocks by themselves. The same is true of drawing. Most one-year olds color and paint only briefly, but some are fascinated with this form of play. Our suggestions are only starting points to send parent and one-year old in a certain direction, but the details of the trip will not emerge until it is underway.

# Suggested Activities

## Water Play

Of all the materials that toddlers explore, water seems to be the most interesting and versatile. Water play can soothe restlessness, dissipate whininess, or heighten excitement. Some situations, like playing in the bathtub, require parental supervision, but many forms of water play allow toddlers to play independently for long periods of time. The following pictures suggest the variety of activities that are possible.

Water with pots and pans

Pouring in the bathtub

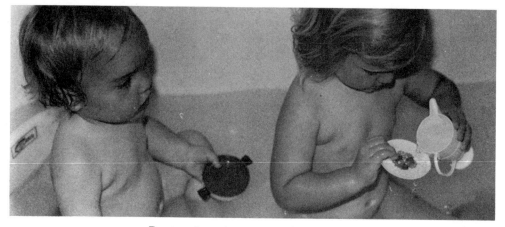
Pretend cooking in the bathtub

Filling the wading pool

Playing with a floating bridge
in the wading pool

Washing toys with soap bubbles

Water painting

Washing rocks in a bucket

Washing a big wheel

Playing with a hose

## Part II
# DAILY LIVING

# Introduction

The Scene:     The dining room in Grandmother's house.

Grandmother:     "Now, Gina." (Picking up Gina who is 15 months old.) "How would you like to sit in this nice new highchair?"

Gina:     "Mommy!"

Grandmother:     "I guess she's not used to me yet. You better put her in the highchair."

Mother:     "No, that's not the problem. She thinks she's too big for a highchair." (The crisis is averted by putting a telephone book on a dining chair.)

LATER:

Grandmother:     (Responding to Gina's whining.) "What's the matter, honey? Would you like a glass of milk?"

Mother:     "No, I think she's had it. I'll take her to the other room and nurse her."

Gina, like all one-year olds, is ambivalent about growing up. At dinner time, she wanted to be big like everyone else and she rejected the highchair emphatically. After dinner, she enjoyed the comfort of breast feeding, and, in this respect, had no interest in being grown-up.

The ambivalence of a toddler puts parents in a double bind. On the one hand, they want their child to reach a new level of independence. On the other hand, they do not want to ignore their child's need for security and nurturance. As parents struggle to achieve an appropriate balance between independence and dependence, there are bound to be some strains in the parent-child relationship. Contributing to the problem is the fact that children do not usually progress in a straight line as they move toward independence. At twelve months, a child may go to sleep quite independently, but several months later start waking in the middle of the night and insist on parental reassurance. A toddler who has been feeding herself may revert to whining and wanting to be fed.

In the next four chapters, we describe routines of daily living shared by toddlers and parents. Caretaking routines associated with sleeptime and mealtime, shopping and housework—all of these are potential opportunities for children to achieve new levels of independence, or to cling to babyish ways.

As children develop new capacities to take an active part in daily routines, conflicts inevitably arise. A conflict may occur when parents expect too much, or when children backslide in their independence. A conflict may result when parents do not take into account a toddler's desire to be grown-up, or when the attempt to be grown-up assumes unreasonable proportions. These conflicts can generate negative feelings on the part of both parents and toddlers. At the same time, daily living with a toddler produces intense positive emotions. We discuss these everyday feelings in the last chapter of this section.

## Chapter 5
# EVERYDAY ROUTINES

Father (to Mother): "Jean, why don't you go and get dressed? I'll give Timmy his supper."

Timothy: "Ghetti - oos."

Father: "Here's your spaghetti. Do you want juice?"

Timothy: "Ye - oos."

Father: "Okay. Here's your glass of apple juice."

Timothy: (Throwing the glass on the floor.) "No oos. No!"

Father: "Timothy, make up your mind. You want milk?"

Timothy: (Shouting) "Want oos."

Mother: (Hearing the shouting, returns to the kitchen.) "Timothy likes his juice in the big bird cup."

Taking care of a toddler is a demanding and time consuming job. In this chapter we focus on prominent caretaking routines, recognizing, of course, that caretaking is never completely routine. It varies from day to day, from situation to situation, and certainly from family to family. But despite these variations, all families with one-year olds share some of the same concerns and face the same kinds of challenges. The purpose of this chapter is to look more closely at the variety of ways families meet these challenges.

In any family with a toddler, it is not unusual to have problems with eating, sleeping, dressing, or some other daily routine. We overheard, for example, a fairly typical conversation between two mothers.

Michael's mother: "You are lucky Veronica eats so well. My Michael is such a picky eater, he drives me crazy."

Veronica's mother: "Who cares about eating? It's sleeping we're having a problem with. Your Michael at least sleeps through the night."

Immersed in a crisis over a particular routine, parents may lose perspective and forget how much progress their children are making. The toddler period is a time of transition, when children grow from helpless infants to surprisingly self-sufficient two-year olds. Sleeping, eating, and other routines gradually change as the children take on more responsibility for self management. Naturally, progress is uneven and all children regress at times. But if parents can keep in mind this larger pattern of development, they may avoid exaggerating the significance of specific problems.

# Sleeping

Going to sleep seems to be the most habit forming of all routines. By the time children are one year old they already have a well established routine that helps them relax and fall asleep. For some children this routine is short and simple—a bath, a bottle of water or milk, a goodnight kiss, and then into their crib. In other families a different pattern is present. Ever since the children were infants, going to sleep has been a time of emotional intimacy between parents and children. The children have been rocked or nursed for an extended period before being placed in the crib. Often the parents have developed the habit of singing to the children, watching television or talking quietly with them.

In families where going to sleep is treated matter-of-factly, relatively few sleep problems are reported. The children may go through brief stages of resisting bedtime, but for the most part they go to sleep easily once they are in bed. In families where bedtime is associated with intimate interaction, there is a greater likelihood of procrastination. Because of the extended contact that precedes bedtime, the children may be more distressed by the eventual departure of parents. They may even try to stay awake in order to prolong the interaction.

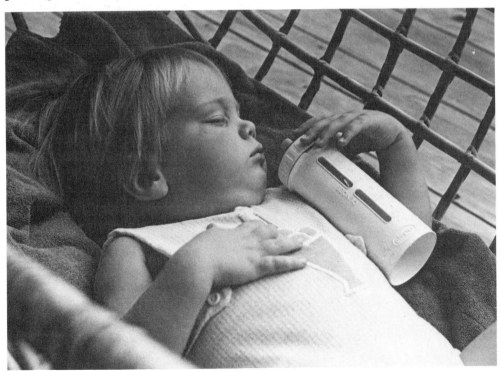

Regardless of their philosophy, parents discover some techniques that help one-year olds accept bedtime. A common technique is to include a stuffed animal in the bedtime routine. In the simplest form of the ritual, parents just give the child a stuffed animal when they say goodnight. Often the routine becomes more elaborate. In Kenneth's family, for example, Stuffy Bear participates in the entire bedtime preparation. First Stuffy Bear puts on his pajamas, then he gets his teeth brushed, and finally, if he has been a very good bear, he can have a little sip of water. Samantha has three favorite stuffed animals, and the family has developed a routine of kissing each animal goodnight. First, Samantha's Dad gives Pooh bear a last kiss on the nose and places him in bed. Next he kisses Smurf and places him by Pooh; and finally, Rabbit Long Ears gets kissed and placed in bed. Then, as Dad leaves the room, Samantha takes her turn kissing each "huggy" goodnight.

A second technique many parents use is reading a bedtime story. The children get ready for bed, select a book, and then sit beside their parent while the story is read. Obviously, the routine becomes elaborated as parents and children share a greater number of stories. If the books are left with the child after the parents leave the room, the children often continue to read by themselves. One-year olds, like their parents, enjoy reading in bed.

Of course, one-year olds find bedtime most acceptable when there is physical contact with parents. Rocking children, nursing them, or holding them, are effective ways to induce relaxation. But a problem may arise when parents try to transfer their children to the crib. The children have grown so accustomed to physical contact that they wake up as soon as the contact is broken. If this kind of bedtime routine is selected the toddler should be transferred before he or she is fully asleep. Although at first there will be more crying, in the long run, independent sleeping will be furthered.

## Changing to a Big Bed

Sometimes parents, with the best of intentions, decide it is time for their toddler to move from a crib to a regular bed. If the child associates this change with being grown-up, the crib may be abandoned without tears. If, however, the child resists the new bed, parents suddenly find themselves in the midst of a sleeptime problem. In this situation parents are best off moving slowly. For a while both the crib and the bed can be left in the room. The child can be encouraged to nap in the bed, while continuing to sleep in the crib at night. When the toddler seems ready to move into the bed at night, the crib blanket and other accessories can be taken along.

Exchanging a crib for a bed is a big change for toddlers and should be planned when other big changes are not taking place. Julia's parents told us about a mistake they made when they moved to a new house. Julia had been involved in setting up her room in the new house and seemed excited about everything: her closet with shelves, the Disney World curtains, and her own big bed. Moving day went fine until bedtime. As her father put her down in the bed, Julia starting sobbing, "No bed, no night-night, go home." Her parents realized immediately that adjusting to a new house and a new bed at the same time was more than Julia could handle.

# Middle of the Night Problems

Nighttime awakening is a very frequent problem with toddlers. Many children cry out in apparent fright or anger as they sleep. Some parents decide to go to the crib and reassure the child. These parents reason that responding to the crying helps a child feel more secure and sustains the bond of trust. Picking up the child, or simply staying in the bedroom for a few minutes, is usually sufficient. When it is not sufficient, parents are likely to let their toddlers sleep with them. This practice usually works as long as the parents are willing to keep it up.

A second approach that parents use is to let their children cry when they wake up at night. Their hope is that the children will go back to sleep by themselves. These parents reason that responding too quickly will encourage nighttime waking. As evidence, they point to the fact that, after a few days or weeks of sporadic crying, nighttime waking diminishes. Having found that company is not forthcoming, the children learn to get back to sleep on their own.

As with other routine problems, there is no one, correct way to handle middle of the night problems. Children at this age are reassured easily if responded to quickly but, at the same time, responding to every call can establish a habit. The appropriate decision for parents depends on the priorities they have already set. If intimacy at bedtime is a high priority, it makes sense for them to get up and answer the child's call or let the child sleep in their bed. If a straightforward sleep routine is their preference, it makes sense to try letting the child cry it out. Whatever their style when putting a one-year old to bed in the first place, it seems best to continue that approach in the middle of the night.

There are times, however, when the approach that parents prefer does not work, and nighttime awakening increases steadily. This situation seems to occur most often with breast-fed children, who may get up every hour or two for a few moments of nursing. Marietta's parents told us the following saga. When Marietta began waking up several times a night, both mother and father tried everything in the book to dissuade her from nursing: offering her a cup of warm milk, turning on a radio in her room, buying her a new stuffed animal to sleep with, and putting a night light in her room. Nothing helped. Marietta just screamed until she was nursed. Finally, their pediatrician suggested that they close the door and let her cry. The first three nights were terrible, but by the fourth night Marietta slept through the night without a whimper.

Although the decision to let a child cry it out is difficult to make, it is not necessarily wrong. If a toddler's sleeping habits are out of hand and the family is exhausted, it is important for parents to assert more control. At the same time, it must be remembered that bedtime problems and sleeping routines are never completely controllable. Parents may prefer a straightforward routine, while their child pushes for an extended period of interaction before going to sleep. Parents may introduce the idea of reading a bedtime story, only to find that their child is not interested. Despite parents' ability to guide sleeping routines, the eventual outcome in any particular situation will be a collaborative effort between parent and child.

# Eating

In the first year babies are hungry at fairly predictable times and they show little evidence of strong likes and dislikes. Parents are in charge of the baby's limited diet, and creating good eating habits is not an issue. During the second year, all this changes. The children are not as hungry, and their appetites fluctuate erratically. Toddlers express their independence by becoming selective about the foods they will eat. An increased sensitivity to

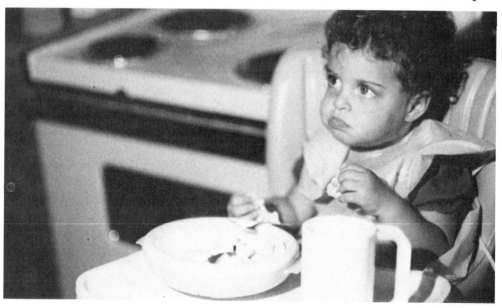

taste and texture leads them to refuse new foods and, if they are slow to master the art of chewing, they may reject meat and other solid foods.

Parents tend to respond to these changes with a new concern over nutrition. They want to be sure that their children eat a well balanced diet, and they hope that the children will sample a variety of foods. Additional clashes may occur over junk food. Although parents can keep junk food away from their toddlers without too much difficulty, the children are beginning to be aware of these food treats. Naturally, parents, in their desire to instill good eating habits, do not want their children "hooked" on foods heavy in salt or sugar.

Parents handle eating conflicts in different ways. Miranda's mother describes her daughter, at eighteen months, as a "finicky eater." Frequently Miranda looks suspiciously at the food on her high chair tray and refuses to try even one bite. Both her parents then introduce some kind of game to get her to eat. The mealtime may begin with, "One bite for Mommy and one bite for Miranda," or Dad's spoon may become a "chug-a-lug-choo-choo" that feeds Miranda while entertaining her.

Rachel, at eighteen months, also goes through spells of eating with enthusiasm and spells of eating very little. Her parents, however, avoid urging her to eat when she is not hungry. If Rachel begins to play with her food or throw it on the floor, her mother takes her out of the high chair. "She'll eat if she's hungry," her mother insists, "and I'm not going to make a big deal over food."

When comparing these two families, it is evident that Rachel's parents are

more relaxed about eating routines. They have decided that prompting Rachel to eat when she's not hungry makes little sense. Instead, they concentrate on giving her a wide selection of nutritious foods, and then leaving the choice about eating in Rachel's hands. In short, Rachel's parents are confident that, eventually, Rachel will self-select an adequate diet.

For parents like Miranda's who find it difficult to be this relaxed about the eating habits of their one-year old, there are other techniques that may smooth over potential conflicts. Food can be cut into very small bites or thin slices. Raw vegetables and fruits, or pieces of meat, are more palatable in this form because the texture and taste are diluted. Parents can suggest a condiment, such as catsup or mayonnaise, for a piece of meat that is ignored by a one-year old. Parents can also provide meat substitutes that require little preparation, like eggs, cheese, or yoghurt. Some parents keep a supply of fish-

sticks or leftover chicken on hand so they can be offered when the family eats something more difficult to chew. A technique that works especially well is to place some of the toddler's food on the parent's plate and have the parent eat it with exaggerated relish.

There is an almost endless variety of ways to make food more appealing, but in every case parents run the risk of overemphasizing the importance of eating. Nowhere is this risk more evident than when parents bribe their children to eat. Offering a treat for eating a nutritional food works in the short run. Soon, however, the children learn to eat the smallest possible amount in order to receive the reward. In general, we would advise parents to be patient when children reject their food. There will be other meals, and the old adage of waiting to try another day is a good philosophy.

Eating routines are also social occasions. During the second year, many parents become concerned about how a child is eating as well as what the child is eating. This is especially true if the toddler is eating dinner with the family. Parents find themselves reminding their children about lapses in table manners. "You don't eat vanilla pudding with your fingers...You don't put your carrot in the milk jug...You don't lick the dish with your tongue."

Although it may not be very evident, one-year olds are making a start toward good table manners. They are learning to use a spoon and fork, and they enjoy using a napkin to clean up messes they have made. If they hear "please" and "thank you" at the table, they may surprise everyone by imitating. More importantly, toddlers are learning that eating routines are a time when the family comes together to share their food and their feelings. Wanting to be a part of this sharing, toddlers may try to join a conversation by yelling louder than anyone else, or try to attract adult attention by performing various antics. With patience and a sense of humor, though, this exuberance can be kept in bounds and mealtime with a toddler can be a pleasant time for interaction.

A final area of conflict related to eating routines is the issue of weaning. While many babies spontaneously give up the breast or bottle at a young age, many other babies are just as insistent on continuing. Parents find a variety of reasons for wanting to wean their children as they become toddlers. Many parents have strong feelings about wanting children to be independent, and they associate a bottle with babyishness. Other parents, who are breast feeding, want to wean their children in order to go back to work. Some mothers have to give up nursing for health related reasons.

When weaning a child from the bottle, parents can make the bottle less attractive by gradually watering down the milk or juice. At the same time, drinking from a cup can be made more attractive by providing an interesting container, or "importing" a peer who is already using a cup.

Weaning breast-fed children is usually more difficult. Experienced mothers tell us that the best way to be successful with weaning is to cut down gradually, stretching out the time between feedings. Abrupt weaning is hard on both mother and child. A question that nursing mothers often ask is whether to bypass the bottle and go directly to the cup. Here, the rationale for weaning comes into play. If the mother wants her toddler to be more grown-up, it is logical to introduce a glass or cup. If the mother gives up nursing for practical reasons, switching to a bottle may be easier. In either case, the child's own preference needs to be taken into account. Where a one-year old shows a definite preference, weaning is a lot smoother if this choice is respected.

# Dressing

For parents, dressing routines represent the process of making a one-year old presentable. This process includes selecting and putting on appropriate clothes, combing and brushing hair, and washing hands and face.

For many toddlers, looking nice is not important. Getting dressed is a bother, and having one's hair brushed or one's face washed is even more senseless. As children approach the age of two, the situation changes slightly. Children adopt a favorite outfit, and they recognize the compliment in words like "pretty" or "cute." They dimly understand that coats and sweaters really are useful in cold weather. It is apparent that a dry diaper feels better than a wet one. Of course, these insights are easy to forget. In the midst of an in-

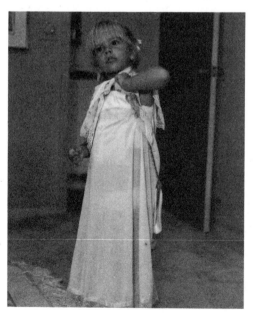

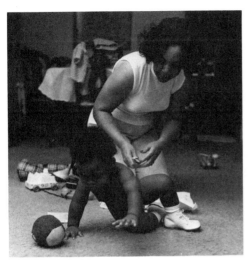

teresting activity, the children are likely to ignore their wet diapers, abandon their coats, and play just as happily without their clothes as with them.

On the days when parents are in the biggest hurry to get the family ready, toddlers seem to be the most resistant toward dressing. They become experts at squirming as their diapers are changed, curling their feet in order to avoid shoes, dodging out of the way when it is time to brush hair, or turning their head from side to side when a parent approaches with a tissue. Parents usually can catch the children, but holding them still and putting their clothes on is another matter. In Timothy's family, when neither watching television nor holding the keys to the car reduced the squirming and twisting, Timothy's father got the idea of placing Timothy in front of a mirror. The idea worked. Timothy got interested in watching the transformation take place as he was dressed. He even tolerated having his hair brushed. For Pamela, getting dressed turned into a game of making choices. "Would you like your Pac-man shirt, or your Strawberry Shortcake shirt?" her mother would ask. Brenan's grandmother took advantage of his burdgeoning sense of humor when it was her turn to do the dressing. "Now, let's see," she began, "I'll put your nose in your sock. Oh, yes, and your shoe goes on your ear." "No, my foot," Brenan laughed, as he helped slide his foot in the shoe.

Perhaps the most effective technique for keeping one-year olds still while you dress them is to sing a dressing song. "This is the way we put on your sock," (sung to the tune of "Here We Go around the Mulberry Bush") is a standard favorite. As the child's ears strain to understand this novel form of communication, the rest of the body relaxes. The dressing routine, instead of being a tiresome interruption, becomes a special occasion.

Singing while dressing a one-year old requires an extra measure of energy, but in the end it is far less of a drain than nagging the child to stay

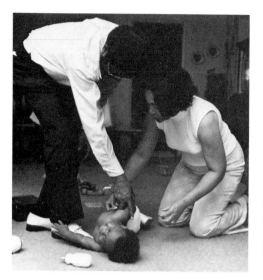 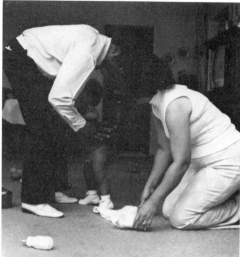

still. Gradually, as toddlers take a greater interest in their personal appearance, they participate more actively in dressing routines. They position their arms and legs to receive the clothes that parents are applying. They may even try to put on certain items of clothing by themselves, such as shoes, hats, or coats.

When all is said and done, however, most one-year olds remain basically disinterested in dressing routines. Their enthusiasm lies in undressing. It is so much easier to take shoes off than to get them back on, to strip off a coat than to put it on. Parents can foster dressing skills in a one-year old by supporting this interest in undressing. Undressing routines can be established just as well as dressing ones. Bathtime, for example, is a prime opportunity for children to take off their clothes and enjoy a brief period of naked cavorting.

# Bathtime

Most toddlers love taking a bath and will stay in the tub for as long as parents will keep an eye on them. Once in a while, however, a one-year old becomes terrified of the bathtub. Parents who face this problem need not feel their children are peculiar. The line between excitement and terror is a thin one. Any exciting activity can quickly become frightening, whether it is a one-year old playing in water, a teenager riding a roller coaster, or an adult speaking in public. Some experience with water has pushed these children over the line, and it takes a long time for them to overcome their fear. A number of alternatives can be tried to entice a fearful child into the bathtub, but the best antidote is arranging for the child to watch other young children taking a bath. Gradually the fearful child can be encouraged to join these peers (cousins are even better) in the bathtub.

The potential scariness of water is quite apparent in the reaction of most toddlers to hair washing. Soap in their eyes on one or two occasions is enough to make hair washing a major ordeal. Some parents have overcome hair washing fears by using a novel container. One mother used a watering can to rinse her child's hair; another parent used a tea kettle. Pretending to wash a doll's hair may help solve the problem. A special song may be reserved for rinsing out the soap, such as "I'm Gonna Wash That Soap (Man) Right Out of My Hair." Once children become fearful, however, parents cannot expect any technique to be immediately successful. As with other fears, time will be needed to convert anxiety back into excitement, and parents need to be willing to experiment with a variety of techniques.

# Toilet Training

Since the advent of disposable diapers, many parents do not even consider toilet training until children are almost two, and even then they approach it with a casual attitude. In general, older toddlers are interested in imitating the behavior of other people, which means that they may enjoy imitating parents and siblings by sitting on the toilet. If a child sits there long enough, this imitation will produce results.

The imitative style of a toddler has other possibilities as well. Gretta, who had little interest in sitting on the potty seat, was interested in toilet training her dolls. Each doll was given a turn on the potty while Gretta made "sss" noises. Although Gretta was emphatic about not sitting on the potty herself, she obviously enjoyed this doll play. As her mother explained, "One day she'll be ready and she'll let us know—at least for now she feels comfortable in the bathroom."

# Baby Sitters

A final topic associated with everyday routines is baby-sitting. Most families find themselves trying to answer such questions as: Should I introduce the sitter ahead of time? Should I leave while my child is awake or wait until he's asleep? Should I make a point of saying goodbye or should I just leave?

Although there are no perfect answers to these questions, guidelines can be abstracted from parent interviews:

1. Give your toddler an opportunity to get to know the sitter while you are at home.
2. Tell your toddler that you are planning to go out even if you don't think he understands.
3. Have a neighbor, relative, or friend serve as a back-up if you are going any distance.
4. Give your baby sitter a list of emergency numbers, including your back-up person.
5. Explain your toddler's sleep routine to the sitter.
6. Get the sitter and your toddler engrossed in a game or book.
7. Say goodbye quickly and matter of factly.
8. Don't look back as you go out of the door.
9. Have a good time.

\*        \*        \*

As you read the sections in this chapter on sleeping, eating, bathing, dressing, and toilet training, you will select ideas that are both pertinent to the problems you are experiencing and compatible with your child rearing beliefs. The daily routine in your family, as in every family, is a reflection of your style and your philosophy as a parent.

Our goal in this chapter has been to demonstate that there are multiple approaches to almost any problem. Although every parent has favorite techniques for managing young children, caretaking problems are minimized when parents remain open to new ideas. At the same time, when parents are struggling to solve a problem, they need to stick with a chosen technique long enough to give it a chance. Flexibility should be balanced with persistence. The secret to this balance is thoughtful communication between caretakers, between mother and father, between mother and grandmother, between friends. Collectively, our caretaking expertise greatly exceeds what any of us can generate independently.

# Suggested Activities

If your toddler has moved into a regular bed, he may have a tendency to wander at night and end up sleeping in your bed. An extra large stuffed animal, although not as reassuring as a parent, can eventually become a satisfactory substitute.

Waving goodbye helps ease the pain of separation. You can give your child a way to say goodbye more intimately by showing him how to blow a kiss. This technique is especially helpful at bedtime. Your toddler gets one last intimate goodbye as you leave the bedroom.

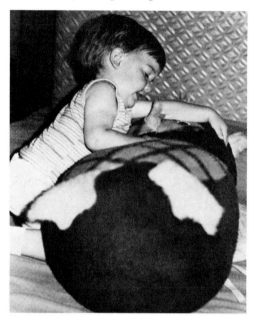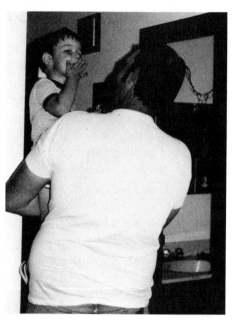

Heading toward the bed when it is bedtime can be a hassle. Try re-enacting the theme of the popular book *Goodnight Moon*. Help your toddler say goodnight to objects as you walk to the bedroom. Pick some favorites, some surprises, some objects outside the window. . . . Goodnight TV, goodnight scotch tape, goodnight dandelions.

Some toddlers naturally develop a habit of playing in their bed before and after sleep. You can try putting different toys and books in your child's bed after he is asleep. Then watch to see if they are played with the next morning. As you discover what appeals to your child, introduce the materials at bedtime and allow your child time to play in bed before falling asleep.

Encourage your toddler to feed herself, whether this means using a spoon and fork, or only fingers. Positive attitudes about eating will be fostered.

If your toddler rejects food that is hard to chew or has a strong taste, this is perfectly normal. You can make such foods more acceptable by cutting them into very thin slices.

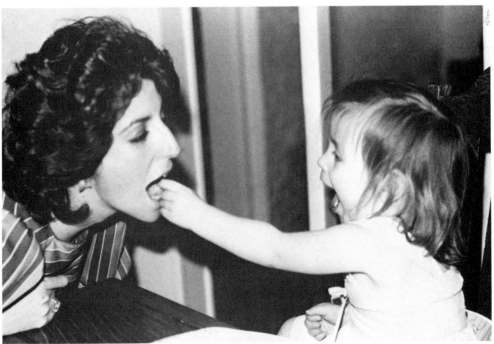

As toddlers become more independent, they like to reverse the usual roles and feed their parents. This is one of many ways that parents and young children can share food. Sharing food does not always mean that toddlers eat more food, but it certainly reduces tension that may be building up at the dinner table.

Before asking your toddler to try a new food, introduce it to a willing dinner guest—a favorite stuffed animal. Naturally the guest will be pleasantly surprised by this new food and heartily recommend it to the child.

Placing your toddler in front of a mirror may help him overlook the inconvenience of having his hair brushed. In fact, he may even begin to see a point to this custom.

Your toddler may be hard to catch when it is time to change clothes. Perhaps he is expressing his independence by refusing to get dressed. You can help him associate independence with dressing by giving him a limited choice of clothing. Having committed himself to one shirt over another, it seems logical to put the shirt on.

Any daily routine is more appealing for your toddler if it is a social occasion. Here a one-year old shares a moment of tooth brushing with an older sibling.

Dressing, like eating, can be played out with dolls and stuffed animals. Although toddlers are not usually able to dress a doll, they certainly can undress it. Stripping the clothes off a favorite stuffed animal is a good prelude for bedtime. First Snoopy gets ready for bed, then Snoopy's friend gets ready for bed.

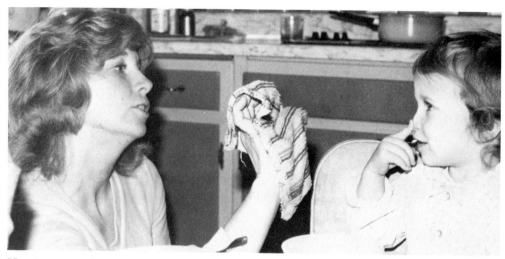

Having your face washed can seem very intrusive to toddlers. If your toddler screams when you approach her with a washrag, transform the washrag into a hand puppet. "Hello, my name is Wendy the Washrag, what's your name?" Soon, your child may be willing to rub noses with this talking washrag.

One-year olds are only beginning to learn how to dress themselves. You can help by encouraging your child to practice any dressing skill that spontaneously arises, whether it is trying on hats, putting one arm in the sleeve of a coat, or struggling to fit a foot into a shoe.

If your toddler is not so sure she wants to sit on the toilet, show her how to put a doll on it. Re-enacting the routine with a doll will help your child learn what is expected and make toilet training more fun.

Once your child has agreed to sit on the toilet, find something interesting for him to do while he sits there. This boy liked to spread skin cream on his legs. Your child may enjoy holding a favorite toy or looking at a book.

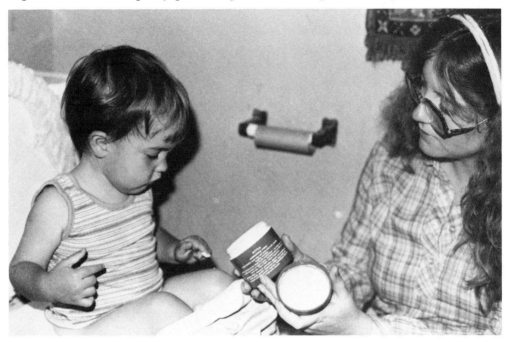

One of the best ways to introduce toilet training is to encourage your child to go into the bathroom with someone else and watch what goes on. Toddlers especially like to accompany friends or siblings who are a year or two older than themselves. You will be surprised what good teachers preschool children can be.

Part of the difficulty in toilet training is getting the child's clothes off in time. Typically parents keep their children in as few clothes as possible when training them in earnest. If it is summertime, and your toddler is ready to be toilet trained, you might concentrate your efforts outside in the back yard. Put a potty chair in the yard, and let your child play naked. Then he or she will always be ready.

Unfortunately, many fathers of toddlers are gone from home most of the day and have little time to interact with their children. One special time that fathers can share with their toddlers is breakfast. If Dad has to leave for work very early, your child can go back to bed for a nap afterward.

Another special time for fathers and toddlers is bedtime. Dad can be the one who specializes in giving the child a bath, putting on the pajamas, and reading a goodnight story.

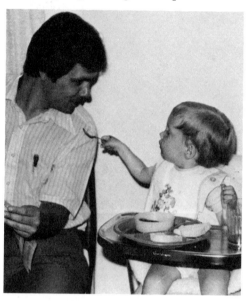

# Chapter 6
# HELPING
# MOM AND DAD

The Scene:  An outdoor barbecue.

Aunt:       "Oh, isn't that adorable. Shannon is helping clean up. She's throwing the paper napkins into the trash."

Shannon:    "De-dee-de-dee, mornin."

Mother:     "She came to help. She's trying to sing, 'This is the way we wash our clothes, early in the morning.' That's what we sing when we do the housework together."

Aunt:       "She's some little girl."

Shannon, having gathered up the last of the used napkins, makes a dive for the package of clean ones.

Mother:     "No-no-no! Those napkins are clean. You do get carried away. Let's put them back in the picnic basket. That's a big girl."

Although a one-year old's efforts to be helpful can sometimes be worse than no help at all, it is fun to watch the performance and natural to praise her effort. In the barbecue scene, Shannon's napkin gathering was reinforced by both Mother and Aunt, and even her attempt to toss out the new napkins was treated with good humor. Shannon made up in enthusiasm whatever she lacked in job skills.

Toddlers are interested in any of the important jobs that adults do. They want to turn on the stereo, drive the car, cut with a knife, write with a pen,

push the lawn mower, and operate the vacuum cleaner. These aspirations, while understandable, are hardly realistic. Having a young child underfoot when you are trying to clean the house, mow the lawn, or cook the dinner is anything but easy. In fact, the more insistent your child is about helping, the more difficult it becomes to accomplish these routine chores.

In this chapter, we will discuss this dilemma by looking at three kinds of housework: doing the laundry, cooking, and cleaning up. Although these three chores encompass only a portion of the household work that parents and toddlers may share, they illustrate how different jobs lend themselves to different degrees of toddler participation. Doing the laundry includes several safe and simple tasks that toddlers can tackle. By contrast, cooking represents a much more dangerous activity in which participation usually is indirect or imaginary. Cleaning up, the third category, is less dangerous than cooking, but usually requires more supervision than typical laundry jobs.

# Doing the Laundry

As we visited different families with toddlers, we found that many of them had found ways to structure laundry chores so that a one-year old could help. In nearly every family, the children were encouraged to put dirty clothes in the hamper, although the consequences were not always what was expected. At Toni's house, for example, Toni's older sister, Gina, came into the living room complaining about having no socks. "Look in the dirty clothes hamper," Toni's mother suggested. Gina went compliantly back into the bedroom. We must have looked puzzled because Toni's mother hastened to add, "Toni loves to help with the laundry, so we always let her put the dirty clothes in the hamper. Sometimes she gets carried away and doesn't wait for the clothes to get dirty." A few minutes later Gina came out with her socks on, confirming her mother's hypothesis.

Sorting the laundry was another activity in which toddlers typically took part. Terry helped sort the dirty laundry into white and colored piles and then enthusiastically threw one pile into the washing machine. Andrea was able to separate the clothes from the dryer into Mom's pile, Dad's pile and Andrea's pile. In sorting the laundry, parents often encountered teasing behavior. The children would unfold the laundry as soon as their parents had it folded, or pull clean clothing out of the drawer as soon as their parents had put it in. Obviously, the children saw no need to draw a sharp line between work and play. In their eyes, sorting and folding laundry was a form of play and teasing was quite appropriate. Parents reported that this kind of situation was made more manageable if the task was organized as a two-step operation. The parents might hand one small, folded item at a time to the child, who then placed it in the drawer. Describing their teamwork helped to keep the rhythm going. "One shirt coming up, one shirt in the drawer . . . another shirt coming up!"

Of course, the most exciting part of doing the laundry is operating the washer and dryer. Under supervision, the children can play the role of assistant operator. They can dump a cup of laundry powder in the washing machine and watch from a safe distance as the tub fills and begins to agitate. They can lend a hand when it comes time to haul the wet clothes out of the washing machine and transfer them to the dryer. They enjoy pushing the "on" button for the dryer and, when the job is done, they like to lean inside the warm, dark hole and fish out the dry clothes. Like many other laundry jobs, operating the washer and dryer involves a lot of emptying and filling. One-year olds can participate easily because the work is a simple extension of a favorite theme in their spontaneous play.

# Cooking

The kitchen is unquestionably the most dangerous spot in the house, and many parents feel that toddlers do not belong in it when food is being cooked. Toddlers, of course, hold quite a different view. In their opinion, the kitchen is a place where interesting things happen and, when Mom or Dad is in the kitchen, that's just where they want to be.

Michael's mother told us there was a firm rule about Michael staying out of the kitchen when dinner was being prepared. "Fortunately, both my husband and I cook, and while one of us does the cooking, the other stays with Michael." Most of the parents we visited, however, did not try to exclude their toddlers from the kitchen. Instead, they concentrated on finding techniques that would keep a young child busy in a safe way. With younger toddlers, the parents provided some floor level distractions while they worked. A favorite distractor was a set of plastic letters, or magnetized objects that stuck

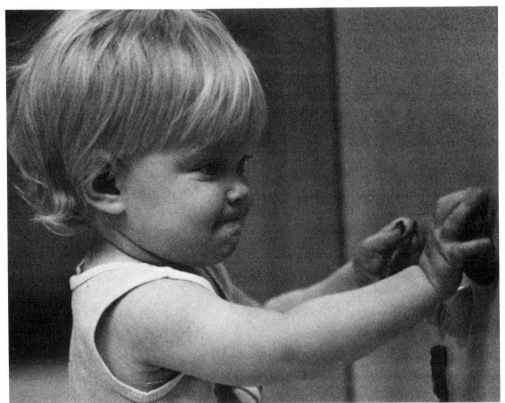

to the refrigerator. (These were put away when parents were not cooking, so they became special toys associated with "cooking time.") Equally successful was a drawer or cupboard that contained kitchen items like pots, pans, spoons and measuring cups. A few families also kept a collection of appealing toys on a low kitchen shelf.

When parents are casual enough in the kitchen to intersperse their cooking with an occasional moment of play, one-year olds may stay in this distractable stage for a long time. The children will develop game routines for the kitchen and they will be satisfied with this degree of involvement. For example, they may develop a game of hiding under the table until a parent finds them, or maneuvering a push toy around and around the table. Their pots and pans play may evolve into pretend cooking, or they may pretend to feed a doll.

Eventually, however, toddlers grow taller and smarter. They notice that dramatic events are taking place on the countertop and stove burners, and they want to see what is going on. Sometimes children can sit on the counter and watch safely. A better solution is a high chair or a sassy seat. (If the sassy seat doesn't fit under the kitchen counter, try pulling out a drawer.) The most versatile watching posture is standing on a sturdy kitchen chair, assuming that the child is now mature enough to stand steadily. The chair can be moved from one vantage point to another.

Watching leads, in time, to wanting to share in the fun, and parents are faced with a one-year old who expects to help cook. Occasionally, children can help with the preparation phase of cooking. A child might join in stirring a cake mix or tearing lettuce for a salad. Parents usually need to redirect their children by offering an activity that has the appearance, but not the substance, of kitchen work. A small quantity of flour and water in a bowl, for example, makes a good mixing job. A wet sponge, a pan, and a dish towel make a toddler feel like part of the work force.

As Julia's mother demonstrated to us, the sink provides an excellent spot for redirecting the energies of older toddlers who want to help in the kitchen.

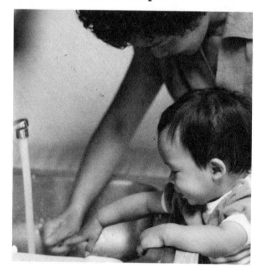

"First, I take off her clothes," Julia's mother began. "Then I fill the sink half full of water, turn the faucets off from underneath and let her play. By giving her a set of measuring cups and some serving spoons, I can get a whole meal prepared while she plays with the water." Other parents described similar discoveries. Detergent, when added to the water, created mounds of bubbles that could be ladled into plastic cups. Turning the water on just a little and letting a toddler play with the drain plug produced an engrossing pastime.

The success of water play at the sink illustrates an important principle. One-year olds are looking for an activity that is intrinsically interesting to them. They want to feel they are involved in kitchen work, but they are not really concerned about the work getting done. Beneath their imitative veneer, the children are most interested in exploratory play. By giving them a chance to explore either by watching, or by manipulating a variety of interesting materials, parents can find a way to accommodate one-year old help in the kitchen.

# Cleaning House

When it comes to housecleaning, parents usually are in favor of having one-year olds help to some degree, especially to begin the habit of picking up their toys. One-year olds, however, seem to be less enthusiastic about this job than about other jobs they see parents doing. For one thing, there is no impressive technology associated with picking up, no buttons to push, no machines to operate. For another thing, children are often told to pick up their toys, which is quite different from volunteering to participate in an adult job.

Typically, children in a school setting are asked to pick up right before a popular activity, and, in this way, picking up becomes a rewarding task. Parents can do the same thing, scheduling a pleasant activity such as reading a story, eating, or going outside, right after picking up. Teachers also use music to signal cleaning up and to set an upbeat mood. A simple song, with made-up verses like, "Clean-up time, clean-up time, now it's time for cleaning," will work wonders with one year old children.

Extra incentives are not always needed for cleaning jobs. One-year olds enjoy scrunching up papers and throwing things in the trash. Even better for some toddlers is the very grown-up task of carrying a trash bag to the garbage can. They can learn to pick up dirty ashtrays and glasses and take them to the kitchen. They like to help clear the table. They can pick up the newspaper and bring it inside, or transfer silverware into and out of the dishwasher. Any of these adult forms of picking up will appeal to a one-year old's sense of self-importance.

Cleaning jobs that involve mechanical picking up are even more popular. Although some one-year olds are frightened by a vacuum cleaner, many toddlers think the vacuum cleaner is the most exciting toy in the house. The children try to turn it on and push it. They sit or stand on it and take a ride. They squat in front of it and dare parents to chase them.

Brooms and mops, although lacking the brute force of vacuum cleaners, also capture the interest of the toddler. These long-handled "creatures" are pretty wild, and one-year olds have their hands full just keeping them in check. Fortunately, parents can substitute child-size versions, and most toddlers are delighted to sweep with a little broom while mother sweeps with the big broom. Child-size vacuum cleaners, carpet sweepers and lawn mowers serve a similar purpose.

Any cleaning job that involves water is appealing. One-year olds are intrigued by the way a sponge soaks up water and are delighted with the task of sponging off the kitchen counter or table top. They enjoy polishing a mirror with water or mopping up spills with a damp cloth. An extra special cleaning job that can be the high point of any toddler's day is helping with the car.

 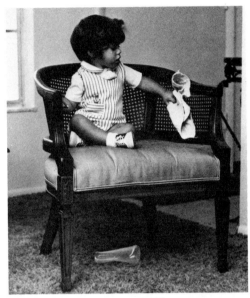

Even cleaning jobs that involve poisonous or caustic chemicals can sometimes be adapted for one-year old participation. One parent told us she puts her one-year old in the bathtub with a squirt bottle of clear water, while she cleans the rest of the bathroom with chemical cleaners. Another parent said she gives her child an empty can of cleanser, which conpensates for not being able to help Mommy with the real thing. Like our suggestions relating to cooking, these examples offer toddlers a kind of pseudo-participation. If, at the same time, they stimulate interesting manipulative play, the children will be content.

\*　　　\*　　　\*

We have discussed three common types of housework, although there are numerous other jobs around the house that toddlers observe and want to try. They see clerical jobs such as typing, paying bills, licking stamps and mailing letters; gardening jobs such as planting, weeding, harvesting and mowing the lawn; construction jobs such as sawing, hammering and painting; and a variety of fix-up jobs. They notice festive jobs, such as carving the pumpkin at Halloween, trimming the Christmas tree, or lighting candles for a special dinner.

Each of these occasions, and many others, presents its own challenge to parents of one-year olds. Is there a way, parents ask themselves, that I can support my child's desire to imitate and be more grown-up, and still get the work done? Perhaps, like folding and putting away the laundry, your child can be given a small piece of the job to perform. Perhaps, like cooking, you can find an exploratory activity that appears to be relevant but does not really interrupt your work. Perhaps you will have to accept the fact that some jobs cannot be satisfactorily completed when an interested toddler is looking over your shoulder.

Toddlers work slowly and inefficiently, and if you are rushing to complete a job, you are likely to feel frustrated. If, on the other hand, you have the time and are not terribly finicky about doing a perfect job, one-year old help may be welcomed. Most parents settle on a middle position. They involve their toddler in housework that both parent and child can enjoy, then save the more hazardous and complicated jobs for times when the child is not around.

Whatever options you select, think through the "costs and benefits" ahead of time. The inconvenience involved in working with a one-year old may be considerable, but the rewards can be even greater. You and your toddler will experience a special kind of intimacy while working together. As you demonstrate a new skill, you will see your child's determined effort to imitate, and when the task is done, you will share in your child's feeling of accomplishment.

# Suggested Activities

Many one-year olds want to help run the vacuum cleaner. Vacuum cleaners do make fine playthings, assuming you can supervise a toddler who is playing with one. When you want to get something accomplished with the vacuum cleaner, however, you probably will need to find an alternative activity for your child. Some children are happy to imitate with a toy vacuum cleaner; another possibility is to give your child a different piece of equipment. A feather duster, or a child-size mop like the one in this picture, is suitable for toddler helpers.

One-year olds are fascinated with squirt bottles, although they may not be able to squeeze the trigger until they are almost two. Because most squirt bottles contain caustic or poisonous liquids, your child's participation is necessarily limited. If your child can operate a squirt bottle by herself, you might give her a bottle that has been filled with plain water. Then, while you use the chemical cleaners, your child can clean with water.

Loading the dishwasher is another adult job that intrigues toddlers. If you are using plastic dishes, your child's help poses no problem. If the dishes are breakable, the situation is different. Some parents show their toddlers how to put silverware in the dishwasher, while they handle the glasses and dishes. Other parents encourage their one-year olds to work on a related cleaning job, such as wiping off the counter or a high chair tray. Try asking

your child to sit on the kitchen floor and wipe off the placemats while you load the dishwasher.

Virtually all toddlers like to throw trash and garbage in a wastebasket. You can extend this "picking up" behavior in many ways. Perhaps your child would be able to help clear the table, bringing leftover food and dirty dishes to the kitchen counter.

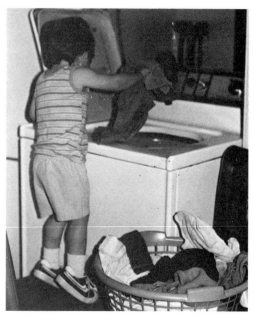

Doing the laundry is a cleaning job that permits a high level of toddler participation. Putting dirty clothes in a hamper is much like throwing trash in the wastebasket. Standing on a sturdy chair, your child may want to transfer the clothes to the washing machine or, at a later point, pull them out of the dryer. Some toddlers help put clean clothes in drawers or linen closets. Perhaps your family has a special spot for coats, such as a big chair by the front door, or a collection point for shoes. Your one-year old will enjoy keeping these hard-to-find clothes in order.

Cooking with a toddler nearby can be hazardous. You can minimize this danger by encouraging your child to play in a safe spot in the kitchen. Younger toddlers are still fascinated with pots and pans, and they like to investigate kitchen cupboards. You might choose one cupboard which is not in the area of the stove, and open it for investigation only during cooking times. Another possibility is to purchase a set of magnetic decorations for your refrigerator and reserve them for cooking times. When you are ready to cook, take the decorations out of a drawer and let your toddler play with them.

With an older toddler, the best technique for distraction in the kitchen is water play. Let your child stand on a chair and play at the kitchen sink while you cook at the stove.

When you are mixing food at a counter, your toddler can sit on the counter and watch from a safe distance. Giving him a whisk or spoon will help him feel a part of the action.

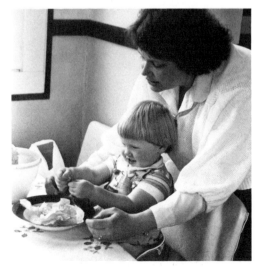

Tearing lettuce for a salad is a safe cooking activity for a one-year old. Naturally you will have to demonstrate at first, but soon your child will be able to do this job independently while you chop the other ingredients.

Under close supervision, toddlers can be allowed to help stir food that is cooking. The best stirring projects, of course, are ones that do not involve cooking, such as stirring instant pudding.

There are a variety of outdoor jobs in which toddlers like to participate. Here are three examples.

Washing the car.

Mowing the lawn with a toy mower.

Watering outdoor plants with a sprinkling can.

# Chapter 7
# GOING OUT IN PUBLIC

| The Scene: | Mother is shopping in a grocery store while Allen, a 21 month old toddler, fidgets in the front seat of the cart. |
| --- | --- |
| Allen: | (In a loud determined voice) "Down." |
| Mother: | (Attempting to distract Allen.) "Look over there. See the pretty stack of toilet paper rolls?" |
| Allen: | "Down, down, down!" |
| Mother | "Okay, you can help Mommy push the cart. Not too fast, now." |
| Allen: | "Allen push." |
| | (At this point, Allen drives the cart into the toilet paper tower, and the whole stack comes tumbling down.) |
| Mother: | (Obviously flustered.) "Oh, no Allen! I told you to be careful. Now you've got to get back in the cart." |

The rules of behavior change when people go out in public. Adults try to be on their best behavior, and interaction tends to be somewhat formal and restrained. One-year olds, of course, have little understanding of this fact of life. For them, public outings are new experiences that produce strong feelings. A child who is basically timid may be overwhelmed by the fast pace of a shopping excursion. The child's reaction to this over-stimulation is to whine, cling, and insist on being carried. A more adventurous child like Allen can create the opposite kind of problem, refusing to sit quietly in a grocery cart or stroller.

Feelings both of excitement and anxiety are to be expected from one-year olds in public. Although neither fits the self-controlled, polite mode that is the adult norm, parents can learn to adapt to their child's public style. Gradually they learn how to comfort an anxious toddler or calm down an over-exuberant one. Even a child who is determined to have some forbidden thing, or get into something that is off limits, can often be distracted. One-year olds are genuinely interested in new people and places and therefore public outings with toddlers can turn into positive experiences most of the time.

# Riding in the Car

The starting point for an excursion is generally a trip in the car, and the first potential problem is strapping the toddler into the car seat. Parents who occasionally make concessions and allow the baby to sit in their laps can

 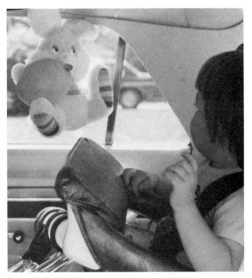

anticipate periodic bursts of temper. Parents who never give in when it comes to the car seat are likely to have an easier time enforcing the car seat rule.

Once the children are strapped securely into the car seat, the problem is to keep them contented. Fortunately for parents, many toddlers are put to sleep by the movement of the car. Other children are quieted by a snack they can hold in their hands or a toy that is tied to the car seat.

At some point during the second year, children develop an interest in looking out of the car window. They may be mesmerized by the moving landscape, staring out of the window without making a sound. They may play a more active role, searching the scene for familiar sights and shouting excitedly when a landmark comes into view. Brian was interested in looking for McDonald's, Kori hunted for garbage trucks, Benjamin, for no obvious reason, shouted "WA-WA" whenever he saw a Chevron sign. Parents can try to extend this kind of game by pointing out objects to their children. Unfortunately, the object is often out of sight by the time the child looks in the right direction.

The most relaxing, enjoyable and fail-safe system for amusing toddlers in a car is singing a song. Car rides and toddlers' memories both lend themselves to songs that have repetitive refrains and verses that go on forever, such as "Old McDonald Had a Farm." McDonald can have a clock that ticks, a tiger that roars, a church bell that clangs, or an engine that goes "vrum-vrum." An acceptable substitute for a sing-along parent is a cassette tape of familiar songs.

# The Issue of Security Objects

Many a trip with a toddler has been delayed on account of a security object. A favorite blanket is in the washing machine, or a dearly loved rabbit was last seen in the kitchen. Parents are usually tolerant and even amused by a young toddler's attachments. But as the child approaches two, many parents have mixed feelings, especially if the object has to go on every outing. The search for the dearly loved rabbit is becoming tiresome, and return trips to the grocery store to retrieve a tattered blanket can precipitate a family squabble. Bottles and pacifiers are especially troublesome. On the surface, parents express concern about their children's teeth. A more basic concern is the meaning they attach to their child's behavior. "If my child needs a pacifier every time we go to the store," parents wonder, "does this mean that he's insecure and I'm an inadequate parent?"

Parents, of course, have the option of making sure that security objects are not taken on public outings. They can insist that such objects remain in the car, or they can refuse to let children take them on trips in the first place. Before adopting such restrictions, however, parents need to consider whether their children will act any more grown-up in public without security objects. Much of the time the children cannot predict whom they are going to meet or what is going to happen next in a public situation. The strangeness of the situation understandably creates some feelings of insecurity. One-year olds without security objects in hand (or mouth) may look more mature at first glance, but it is doubtful that they actually feel more secure. In fact, it is likely that the children feel most confident and outgoing when supported by their security objects.

If parents are bothered by the sight of a pacifier in the mouth of their one-year old, or if they think it is time for the child to stop drinking a bottle in public, they can encourage their children to substitute other security objects. Dolls and stuffed animals are traditional favorites. As children grow older, these objects provide better companionship than a pacifier or a blanket, and they are more acceptable to adults. A one-year old who is beginning to recognize the characters on "Sesame Street," for example, may adopt a muppet doll for public outings. Or the child might form an attachment to a stuffed animal that resembles a character in a storybook. Some one-year olds enjoy taking an accessory on a public outing, such as a purse, a set of keys, jewelry, hats, or sunglasses. In time this kind of object may serve a security function. Other one-year olds express a desire to carry along toys. Once again, parents are in a position to help children select objects that will be relatively easy to manage. By responding to the interests of their children, parents can suggest toys that promote new forms of play while providing emotional support.

# Limiting Exploration in a Store

One-year olds often feel insecure in public, but they also like to explore new territory. At a store, the children may want to handle the merchandise and venture down the aisles by themselves. Instead of worrying about the use of security objects, parents become concerned about how to manage their children's exploration. In fact, shopping in a store may turn into a new kind of game for one-year olds. They run away and parents chase them, they hide and parents find them.

As frustrating as such moments can be for parents, they are a sign of growth. The children want to be involved in what is going on, and sooner or later parents find themselves helping the children define an active role that is acceptable. Whether this process takes place sooner or later depends on several factors. How often is the child taken on public outings? How urgent is a child's desire to explore in public? Is the child able to climb out of a stroller of shopping cart?

Perhaps the most important variable is the pattern that has already been established at home. If children are permitted to explore most objects at home, they will want to touch and handle things in a store. Parents may wish that their one-year olds were active explorers at home and circumspect shoppers in public, but it usually does not happen that way. Encouraging exploration at home means that parents have to work harder supervising their children in public.

Some parents avoid the problem by not taking their children to stores at all. Other families include two parents on shopping trips. One parent does the shopping and the other watches the child. For most parents, however, these options are not available. They need techniques that take into account the desire of one-year olds to be more active while at the same time permitting shopping to be completed with a minimum of hassles.

Perhaps the most common technique is to stimulate visual exploration. When one-year olds are busy looking at things, they may be willing to stay in a stroller or shopping cart. In a grocery store, the shopping cart is moving most of the time and children are seated high enough to see all the shelves. Pointing out the variety of interesting sights as they pass by will hold the children in their places relatively well. At a mall, where childen are seated in strollers low to the ground, and where the strollers stop for extended periods, children grow restless more quickly. Parents can try to alleviate this boredom by parking the stroller in a spot with a good view. The stroller might be placed in front of a window or a mirror, especially a three-panel mirror. It might be positioned so that the child can look inside a jewelry case or see some other children playing. While waiting for a sales clerk, parents can seat toddlers on the counter. From this vantage point, the children can watch the exchange of money and marvel at the mystery of a computerized cash register.

If looking is supplemented by touching, the chances of keeping children in a stroller or shopping cart are even better. Again, the grocery store provides the best examples. Children can eat while they sit in the cart — in fact, what could be more natural when surrounded by every imaginable kind of food? One-year olds can be given certain foodstuffs to hold on their laps, or they can drop these items in the back of the cart. They can hold a shopping list or a deli number. At the checkout stand, despite the presence of items that parents do not want to purchase, there are many opportunities to touch and hold objects. A toddler can help put food on the conveyor belt, hand money or coupons to the clerk, carry a bag with a special food in it, or hold a new magazine that is being bought.

Eventually, of course, children will insist on getting out of the stroller or shopping cart. After all, everyone else in the store is free to walk around and investigate. However, even when children reach this point, sometime between the ages of one and three, the stroller or shopping cart can be used to structure their exploration. Instead of confining children inside the stroller or shopping cart, parents can encourage them to take over the job of pushing these vehicles.

First attempts at steering are not without peril. One-year olds do occasionally crash into a display of merchandise or into another shopper. But it is much easier for parents to supervise children who stay with a stroller or shopping cart than children who roam foot-loose and fancy-free. In the grocery store, the shopping cart is an integral part of the shopping process and, therefore, its driver becomes integrated into the process as well. Similarly, in a department store a stroller can become part of the shopping process. Children can be allowed to put purchased merchandise in the stroller.

This strategy can, of course, backfire. Children end up putting unwanted items in the stroller, and they are opened or torn up before they get back on the shelf. Rachel's mother found that it cost her five dollars to get a thirty-five cent birthday card. A less costly alternative is to encourage a one-year old to take a doll or stuffed animal to the mall and give it a ride in the stroller. After pushing for a while, the child often gets tired and is willing to sit in the stroller for the rest of the shopping trip.

# Shopping Rituals

Shopping is a routine most of the time. Parents and children often discover looking and touching opportunities that become part of the routine. Jessica, at fifteen months, was fascinated by a Big Bird mannequin in one

of the stores at the shopping mall. Recognizing her fascination, Jessica's mother made a visit to Big Bird the high-point of going shopping. Whenever Jessica began to get restless, Jessica's mother would say, "Oh, it's almost time to see Big Bird." Other shopping rituals that parents described to us included a ride on a mechanical horse, a visit to a store window with a giant Raggedy Ann doll, and a trip up and down an escalator.

Shopping rituals are compromises. They are a way of accommodating the interests of the child, while giving the parents time in between to get the shopping done. Of course, one-year olds hardly comprehend the contractual nature of such bargains, and parents can have difficulty convincing them that a ritual must come to an end. From the child's point of view, the fun should go on forever.

Some parents seek a happy conclusion by holding up one finger and telling the child "one more minute." Even though the child does not know how long one minute is, this advance warning may make the ending acceptable. Other parents capitalize on the power of waving "bye-bye." When it is time to go, they tell the child to wave "bye-bye" to whatever is being left. Parents can try to end a shopping ritual through distraction and humor. A new idea can be introduced, calculated to attract the child's attention and to facilitate a quick departure. For example, a parent might end a ride on a McDonald's merry-go-round by saying, "Now let's go outside and look for the moon," or "Let's go home and give your teddy bear some milk—your teddy bear is very hungry."

# Managing Your Own Embarrassment

When there is parent-child conflict in public, for whatever reason, parents tend to react in one of two ways. Either they hustle the children out of the store, often carrying them in their arms, or they punish the children more severely than is their custom. In a word, parents panic. They over-react because they are embarrassed. Often they assume that other adults are watching them and making critical judgments.

The truth is that other adults generally pay little attention to a one-year old who is having a tantrum. Many of the shoppers have had the same experience with their own children and realize that such behavior is not unusual. The onlookers also have other matters on their minds. In general, their response is neutral but sympathetic. A minority of onlookers may make negative judgments and, unfortunately, they are the ones most likely to voice their sentiments. Parents, being in an agitated state, wrongly conclude that these disapproving glances or critical comments represent the majority's opinion.

Feelings of embarrassment are perhaps most likely when a toddler is taken to a restaurant. In many restaurants, children are expected to stay in their seats, to talk in hushed tones, and to wait patiently for the meal to be served. Toddlers who don't mind staying still may have little difficulty with these rules, but children who like to move around are going to be fussy and restless. Surrounded by other adults who are enjoying a leisurely dinner, parents find themselves getting tense and angry.

Some parental feelings of embarrassment and anger are to be expected when a one-year old is taken to a fancy restaurant. Many parents stay with family restaurants or fast food spots until their children are older. Other parents take along a restaurant pack with favorite toys, a book, or perhaps a snack to help with idle time. Timothy's parents made a point of talking to the diners at the neighboring table before sitting down. "This is our boy, Timothy," his father would say. "I hope he is not going to bother you." Prepared for some overexuberance, the neighboring diners became friendly and helpful, and Timothy's parents could usually enjoy a peaceful dinner.

\*     \*     \*

No matter how inventive parents are in finding ways to make public outings pleasant, adults act differently in public than at home and children pick up the difference. On the one hand, parents are more lenient. They will carry a whining child or respond to a groundless temper tamtrum. On the other hand, the behavioral rules are more stringent. Children cannot go whooping through the supermarket, sing a raucous song in a restaurant, or rearrange the display in a dress shop.

Fortunately, both parents and children learn to adjust to the special demands of a public outing. Exploratory children accept the extra restraint, knowing that their parents will give them some extra attention. Timid children adjust to the added insecurity, knowing that their parents are always there to keep them safe. Parents become more tolerant of a young child's public behavior and are less likely to be embarrassed by outbursts or indiscretions. As parents relax, so do their children, and the balance between tension and enjoyment that characterizes a public outing tips to the side of enjoyment.

# Suggested Activities

## Getting Started

If leaving the house is a problem, try asking your toddler to carry an important object, like Mom's purse, out to the car.

Many one-year olds like to take a stuffed friend with them on outings. If you want your toddler to leave the friend in the car, create a pretend conversation. "O.K. Friend, don't worry. We'll be back to play with you soon."

If car trips are a problem, try fastening a steering wheel toy to the car seat. Children like to share the driving.

## At the Grocery Store

Your child may enjoy helping you put items of food into the grocery cart. Talk about each item as you take it off the shelf.

The check-out counter is every parent's nemesis. Not only do you have to wait in line, but the area is crowded with last minute temptations, most of which you will not want to buy. Often, however, there is some small item that you would not mind purchasing. Before you reach the check-out counter, make your decision and tell your child that now it is time to get a magazine, a package of gum, or whatever. Then encourage your child to hold this item and hand it to the cashier. Soon your child will anticipate having this job. If you decide not to get anything at the check-out counter, hand your child a foodstuff from the grocery cart and ask him to give it to the cashier.

# At the Mall

One way to encourage your child to stay in the stroller is to park it in an interesting spot, such as in front of a mirror or an outside window. When shopping for clothes, leave the stroller near a clothes rack so that your child can touch the merchandise.

One-year olds have a habit of running away while you are waiting at a counter. You can keep your child contented and close at hand by seating him on the counter. From this new vantage point, he will see interesting things and be in a position to interact with other adults.

An older toddler who wants to imitate you will enjoy shopping with his own basket or shopping bag. Simply carrying such a symbol of consumerhood will be sufficient at first. Gradually the child may start to fill the basket with items. You can pre-empt this option by giving your child some merchandise you have selected.

When your child no longer will accept sitting in the stroller on shopping trips, encourage him to push the stroller instead. Putting a doll in the stroller and talking to your child about taking care of the doll makes the job more realistic and appealing. You still will be directing your child this way and that, but your comments will seem more like those of a companion than an authority figure.

Intersperse in your shopping routine a few brief activities that are strictly for your toddler's benefit , such as making a regular visit to an enticing display.

When you take a break from your shopping to play for a few moments, it is sometimes hard to end the break and get back to business. One of the simplest and most effective ways to terminate an activity is to say "goodbye" to it. The act of waving goodbye is a powerful ritual that one-year olds can hardly refrain from joining. It gives them a means of saying, "I'm sorry, but

I have to go now," while holding out the promise that someday they may return.

# At a Restaurant

If you like to go out to eat but fear your toddler will be a pest, try breakfast at a restaurant. The atmosphere is more casual at breakfast time, and your child is likely to be both hungry and refreshed.

When you go to a restaurant where there will be a delay before the food is served, bring along appetizers for your toddler. Try finger foods that encourage your child to eat slowly. For example, place a handful of Cheerios in a row so that your child will pick them up and eat them one at a time. Give your child a little box of raisins which she can fish out on her own.

Children who like to eat are usually contented in a restaurant, for eating is the objective of the outing. Children who would rather play are not entertained so easily. In some restaurants, parents may feel comfortable letting their children run around near the table. If your child is the explorer type and you want to keep him at the table, you will need to provide something worth exploring. Bring along an old purse filled with small toys or household items that interest your child. Let him open this surprise package and play with the contents. Remember that one of the most time consuming and enjoyable activities is simply moving the objects in and out of the purse.

Finger plays are a good way to keep your child occupied while waiting to be served. The following jingle allows for some creative variations which can be sung while sitting at the table.

"Rabbit is coming with a hop, hop, hop.
He's hopping on my hand and he will not stop.
He's hopping on my thumb and my finger too.
Hop away, Rabbit I've had enough of you!"
  (on my shoulder and my tummy too, etc.)

# Chapter 8
# EVERYDAY FEELINGS

Kathleen: (Pulling at the refrigerator.) "Milk."

Daddy:   "Good talking. I'll get you milk. Here's your cup of milk."

Kathleen: (Holding cup and trying to climb on kitchen chair. Spills milk.) "Uh-oh."

Daddy:   "'Uh-oh' is right. Now you help Daddy wipe it up. This time Daddy will give you milk after you're sitting in the chair."

Kathleen: (Now sitting in the chair, spills the milk deliberately.) "Uh-oh."

Daddy:   "No, Kathleen, that was naughty. You don't spill milk on purpose."

Kathleen: (In a questioning voice.) "Daddy mad?"

Underlying the hustle and bustle of family life with a one-year old is a whole range of shared emotions. In fact, the interplay of feelings between a parent and toddler is the most central characteristic of their daily routine. Each one is adjusting to the temperament and personality of the other, and the attachment bond, which was formed during the child's infancy, takes on new dimensions. In a manner of speaking, you and your child are growing both closer and further apart.

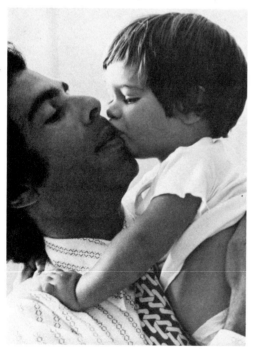

# Resistance and Temper Tantrums

For many parents, the change in their toddlers' emotional tone that both surprises and concerns them most is the appearance of defiance. In a predictable fashion, one-year olds begin to say "no" during the second half of the second year. With this one small word, the children find they can resist any suggestion or directive. Actually there probably have been non-verbal signs of resistance for some months. Young toddlers know how to emphatically reject a bite of food by pushing the spoon away, or how to resist being held by stiffening their bodies. The ability to resist with language, however, opens up a new vista, and for several months it may seem that the child can think of nothing else. "No" becomes an automatic response to almost every situation.

Frequently it is hard to tell just how serious one-year olds are when they act defiantly. Do they really mean "no," or are they just testing the limits of their new found power? Parents usually conclude that the best strategy is to treat an outburst of negativism as casually as possible. They may offer a brief explanation to support a request or they may make a reasonable compromise; much of the time they just proceed as if they had heard nothing.

Annoying as the toddler's negativism can be, it is also a source of satisfaction for parents. Resistance is a sign of independence, an indication that children want to do things for themselves, be their own persons. More specifically, the negativism of toddlers shows that the children are becoming aware of the scope of human decision-making. They are beginning to realize that daily routines are not fixed by law or nature. Routines are decided upon by individuals, and one-year olds want to be included in the process. At first, because their understanding is so limited, the children see only the possibility of resisting the decisions of others. In time, they go beyond this initial step and find other more positive ways to take part in decision-making.

Between the ages of one and two, many children also display their first genuine temper tantrums. The children have been angry before, but as their ability to anticipate becomes more precise, they feel disappointment more keenly. Clearer expectations mean that frustration is that much sharper. At first these feelings of anger are directed mostly at objects. A toy is stuck behind a chair, or a puzzle piece won't go in. Increasingly, though, some of the children's anger is directed at parents: Mom won't open the refrigerator door or Dad cuts a french fried potato in half when son likes his potato left whole.

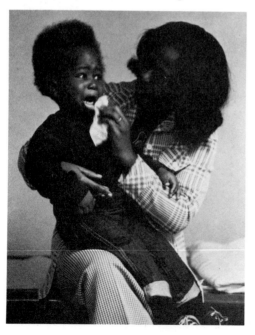

Like other forms of negativism, parents find that it is better to ignore these tantrums than to try consoling their children. The tantrums are short-lived and the mood of the children quickly changes for the better. As a matter of fact, a toddler's temper tantrum may have a comic quality because toddlers are not too adept at pounding and screaming.

Tantrums, at any age, are most likely to occur in the presence of trusted adults. Recognizing that the tantrum is not just taking place in a vacuum, but is directed at them, each parent responds in a characteristic way. Some parents ignore a tantrum as it is occurring, but are quick to comfort their children after the tantrum subsides. They feel that tantrums are an expression of legitimate feelings and that angry children need help in calming down. Other parents are more punitive in their reaction to tantrums. They are convinced that tantrums are a sign of a difficult child and they want to nip this behavior in the bud. In actuality, too much attention to a tantrum, whether the attention is positive or negative, is likely to be counter-productive. Although it may be difficult to be consistently casual when your child is screaming, it is probably the most effective method of reducing the recurrence of tantrums.

# Feelings of Pride

The tantrum behavior of a one-year old is the negative side of a one-year old's emotional growth. On the positive side, a new sense of independence

and social power is expressed in feelings of pride. Young toddlers proudly bring objects they are investigating to parents. They want to share their sense of discovery. Older toddlers, who are more verbal, ask parents to watch them perform new tricks.

For the most part, toddlers are aware of becoming the center of attention and play the role to the hilt. If an antic like spinning in a circle attracts adult attention, toddlers are quick to perform their repertoire. They may run up to adults with an expectant laugh, stamp their feet in a version of a tap dance, or stick their head between their legs as the starting point of a sommer-sault. If the adult responds to these feats with applause, the toddler is quick to join in.

One-year olds are not insensitive to compliments either. Many a one year old girl takes special pride in donning a new dress or a collection of cos-tume jewelry. And many a one year old boy puffs out his chest or flexes his arm in a demonstration of muscle power. Children of both sexes seize op-portunities to demonstrate their "smartness." Although controversy abounds over whether these traditional patterns can or ought to be changed, the abil-ity of one-year olds to develop feelings of pride is incontestable.

Both feelings of pride and feelings of anger signal an emerging self-awareness in one-year olds. The children are starting to grasp that they are distinct individuals. No longer do they cry automatically when other children are hurt, or become afraid when Mommy washes her hair. Space is opening up between their own experiences and the experiences of others. While this space permits a new level of independence, it also raises the specter of separation. A one-year old who is full of "no's," who proudly demonstrates new skills, is also likely to express fear of separation even when separations are brief.

# Separation

Separation, in various degrees, is an everyday experience for all toddlers. At home, parents see their children gaining the confidence to explore further and further on their own. Suddenly a parent realizes that a child has wandered into an adjoining room and is playing happily by himself. For the first time, a child ventures upstairs unaccompanied and goes to her bedroom to find a toy. In these new situations, parents and one-year olds work together to define an acceptable level of separation. Parents want to keep an eye on what their toddlers are doing, just as the children want to be assured that parents can easily be located.

Separation also occurs at bedtime. In fact, the way parents handle bedtime is a good indication of their general approach to separation anxiety. Some parents make a special effort to settle their children before bedtime by initiating "goodnight" rituals. When leaving their children with baby sitters, these same parents go to extra lengths to explain separation and be reassuring. Other parents, who encourage their children to go to bed without fanfare, treat baby sitter situations in a similar manner.

For many one-year olds, child-care experience represents the most traumatic form of separation. It is not unusual for children to go through several difficult months of adjustment, particularly if they have spent the first year of life in a home setting. Parents can help by maintaining a consistently firm but calm attitude toward the child-care routine. They can allow toddlers to take security objects with them to the place of child-care. (Unfortunately, many child-care centers have a rule against such behavior.) Parents can tell children, in concrete terms, when they will return—"I will pick you up after your nap." They can make leave-taking less traumatic by saying goodbye in a cheerful, non-hurried, but non-hesitant way. Finally, by keeping lines of communication open with substitute caretakers, parents can find out how their children are adjusting. If caretakers report continued signs of depression in their child, such as withdrawn behavior or extended periods of

sleeping, the parents will be in a position to decide whether or not the child's placement needs to be changed.

Separation anxiety at bedtime, with a baby sitter or at a child-care center, is understandable in one-year olds. The children are not sophisticated enough to comprehend why parents must leave them with substitutes. "If you abandon me one time," the children seem to be thinking, "might you abandon me anytime?" Typically, toddlers protest vehemently when a parent leaves, but then calm down a few minutes later. Being overly responsive to the initial protest communicates to the child that the separation experience is indeed going to be frightening. Next time the child screams even louder and

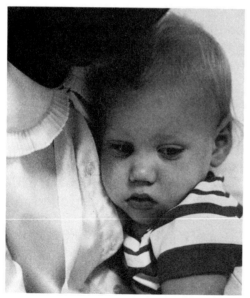
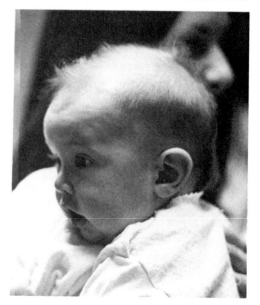

the parent feels more pressure to be reassuring. Such a pattern is counter-productive for both parent and child. It cannot be reversed overnight, but parents who find themselves in this predicament can make a special point of encouraging brief separations in their daily routine. As the parents find other adults or children with whom their child is comfortable, they can arrange longer separations.

Ultimately, a one-year old's sense of separation represents a step forward and an opportunity to develop new relationships. The children are expanding their attachment bonds to include a wider circle of people. Friendships blossom with aunts and uncles, cousins, neighbors, older children, and peers. One-year olds appreciate the different qualities of these new friends, and unique activities and social games come to be associated with each one. Many parents even discover that this is a good time to introduce the idea of staying overnight with a relative or adult friend. Separation can become a positive experience, a chance to feel socially independent. Parents who conclude that an overnight visit would not work for their toddler can still take into account the child's friendships when getting a baby sitter. Allying friendship with separaton increases the probability of a positive experience.

Unfortunately, situations do sometimes arise where a family cannot plan ahead for separation, or where a separation is extended. Toddlers usually react to unplanned or extended separations in a characteristic pattern. Initial crying and protestations give way to a period of acceptance when the toddler appears to be coping well. Then, when the parents return to the home, the toddler reacts with anger or rejection. It may take hours or even days before toddlers forgive their parents for leaving, and harmony is restored. Letting toddlers see photographs of their parents, hear their voices on the phone or on a tape, and wear some piece of clothing or jewelry that belongs to Mom or Dad may make the separation less traumatic.

# The Arrival of a New Sibling

When the reason for separation is the birth of a sibling, your toddler may have an even more difficult period of adjustment. From a toddler's point of view, Mother has not only been absent without leave, but she has also returned home with a substitute baby. This new baby gets gifts from all the visitors, is the center of attention, and has no play value whatsoever. Wendy, at just under two years old, expressed her concern when first introduced to her brother: "Baby come out of tummy? Put it back!"

Fortunately, with rare exceptions, parents have plenty of time to prepare their toddlers for a big brother or big sister role. Although there is no way of eliminating negative feelings towards a new baby, parents can help with the adjustment period through advance preparation. Here are some ideas that parents have shared with us.

Make a scrap book of pictures of baby furnishings including: a cradle or port-a-crib, a crib; a carriage; an infant seat; a diaper bag; and an infant car seat. As you read the scrap book with your toddler, talk about the things "our baby" will need.

Take out your toddler's baby book or photo album, and talk about the time when he was a baby.

Let your toddler help sort out and fold clothes for the new baby.

Help your toddler take care of a baby doll or a baby stuffed animal.

Teach your toddler a lullaby to sing to the new baby.

Let your toddler feel the new baby "pushing" in your uterus. (Avoid talking about the baby kicking. Toddlers don't like babies who kick their mother.)

\*　　　\*　　　\*

In many different ways, the toddler period is a time of strong ambivalence. One minute the children are in the throes of a temper tantrum, the next minute they may be cuddling with parents or playing cheerfully. One minute they insist on crossing the street without holding a parent's hand, the next minute they may whine to be picked up and carried. One-year olds are struggling to balance feelings of independence and dependence. For the first time in their lives, but certainly not the last, they want both the freedom of independence and the security of dependence. The long journey of growing up has begun, and each toddler starts to map out his or her individual path.

Parents respond as individuals also. In each family, independence is encouraged in different ways. Parents may stress independence in the form of self-help skills, learning to use a spoon and fork, a toothbrush, or a washrag. They may emphasize independence by offering choices to a one-year old: what juice for breakfast; what shirt for the day care center, which toy for riding in the car. Parents may promote independence by allowing children to help with adult jobs, such as washing the clothes or cleaning the house. They may take their children on excursions, such as a visit to a petting zoo, a trip to the park, a visit with friends in the country, where the children can explore on their own.

While each family seeks out ways to promote independence, parents are just as concerned with helping their children remain compliant. There are many situations in which toddlers are too young and inexperienced to make decisions for themselves or to act independently. In these situations, parents want one-year olds to remain dependent upon them for supervision. Again, each family reinforces a somewhat different pattern of dependence.

In its own way, every family strikes a balance between independence and dependence. And despite differences in philosophy, all these families can succeed in communicating love to their children. In this chapter we have focused on several specific emotions, especially negative feelings that concern parents of toddlers. These emotions, which are prominent in the burgeoning self-expression of one-year olds, do not exist in isolation. They are part of a complex web of feelings that connects family members. This connectedness begins at birth when infants and parents form an initial bond with each other. As the infants become toddlers, the connections multiply and diversify. The children begin to understand that emotions within a family are played out in a context of belonging. Welcoming a parent home with a joyous smile, or giving a parent an unexpected hug, the one-year old is learning how to say, "We belong together."

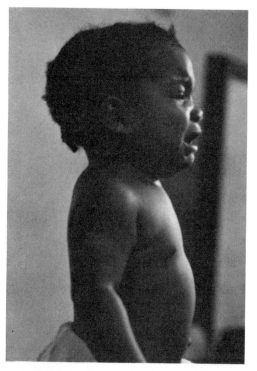
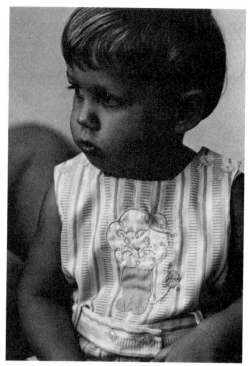
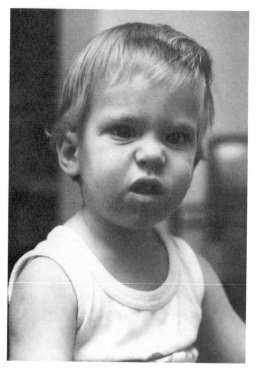

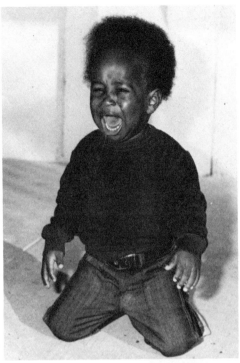

## *Part III*
# PLAYING AND LEARNING

# Introduction

The Scene: Nicholas and his mother are standing on the front lawn waiting for Nicholas' Dad to come home from work. As he arrives, Dad lunges toward Nicholas in a football tackle position, thrusts his head in his son's tummy, and lifts him up into the air.

Nicholas: "More, more." (Kicking his legs and laughing out loud.)

Dad: "All right, all right." (Sitting Nicholas on his shoulders.) "But first let me say hello to your mommy."

Parents enjoy playing this kind of game with their one-year olds. We might call it an "interlude game." For a minute or two, perhaps for only a few seconds, the parent and child share a bit of roughhousing, a ritualistic game,

or a private joke. The parent who hides a candy, first in one hand and then in the other, is subject to a stubborn search. The parent who wears a frisbee like a hat is rewarded with a curious smile. The parent who makes a fierce face and threatens, "I'm gonna get you," is greeted with shrieks of excitement. The children realize the absurdity in a candy disappearing, the incongruity in a frisbee hat, and the utter unbelievability of a parent-monster.

Over the course of the second year parents will watch their children learning how to start the silliness, too. Some jokes are stumbled upon quite by accident, but as soon as the child notices the audience's reaction, the joke is repeated and stored for future use. Many one-year olds, for example, find that a sudden reversion to crawling brings an appreciative laugh from others. Perhaps the child gains center stage by shuffling around in Dad's shoes or by performing a half completed somersault. One-year olds also pick up joke routines through imitation. Seeing the frisbee on Mother's head, a toddler may be inspired to experiment with a variety of headware, such as boxes, pans, and vegetable sieves.

When one-year olds first discover their power to make a joke, they sometimes miscalculate. In hopes of getting a laugh, a toddler may pinch a parent's arm or run away in a store. Mischievous behavior can even become deliberately obstinant. Having discovered that pouring milk on the floor makes Mother lose her temper, the toddler seeks out every opportunity to overturn a drink. Similarly, a toddler may stubbornly continue to pull leaves off a plant, refuse kisses, or mercilessly tease a pet.

Parents, who are sure their toddlers know better, become convinced that their children are being mean on purpose. Usually, however, the children are only testing out the inconsistent responses of parents. All of us tend to smile indulgently when a toddler tries to tease us, but then get angry when the behavior is carried too far. It takes a few months for children to sort out these mixed messages and identify acceptable teasing routines. After a while they recognize that getting a negative reaction from parents, impressive though it may be, is not worth the consequences. Parents go through a difficult period when their children act defiant. With a large part of their time devoted to playing policeman, parents can lose sight of the fun of parent-child play. They may forget how parent-child play nourishes feelings of attachment.

In this section we will look at how parents can keep play alive. By taking the time to play with their toddlers, parents recapture earlier feelings of intimacy and rejuvenate themselves for the next round of conflict. In Chapter 9 we discuss the spontaneous physical games that parents and toddlers can share. Chapter 10 is concerned with toy play, how parents and young children enjoy the most common types of toys: balls, cars, block, and dolls. In Chapter 11 we focus on the relationship between play and language, describing how parents can read books with their toddlers and exploring possibilities for more advanced conversational play. The final chapter in this section looks at play beyond the parent-child dyad. We discuss how play enables toddlers to make friends with peers, older children, and adults other than their parents.

As parents and toddlers share longer and longer play episodes, there is a greater instructional component in the play. Parents have an opportunity to teach children new words, skills and concepts. In addition, parents can introduce their children to the world of imagination. Whether parents are manipulating toys with children, looking at the pictures in a book, or playing a physical game with them, play is more fun when fantasy creeps in.

Although all parents enjoy playing with their one-year old, they go about it in different ways. They have varied play interests and styles of play. Our intent in this section of the book is to help you develop your own style. Knowing more about the kinds of games and play routines that are possible will stimulate your creativity, and both you and your child will gain greater satisfaction from play.

*Chapter 9*
# PHYSICAL GAMES WITH ONE-YEAR OLDS

The
Scene:   A bedroom, early morning. Dad is hiding under the sheet. Mom enters the room carrying Amelia, age eighteen months.

Amelia:   "Where Daddy, where Daddy?"

Mother:   (Placing Amelia on the bed.) "Daddy's not here. Daddy went to New York City."

Daddy:   (Extricating himself from the sheet.) "Peek-a-boo — I see you?"

Amelia laughs uproariously and covers her Dad back up with the sheet.

"Peek-a-boo," that universal favorite of parents and young children, provides an excellent example of the way physical games are changing as infants become toddlers. First, children may draw out the game, even to the point of exhausting their parents. The children have learned to signal when they want "more," and they become increasingly vocal and insistent in demanding that a game be continued.

In addition, familiar routines are evolving into more complex games. Peek-a-boo," for example, leads to "Hide and Seek." This new version of the game may start when a parent hides behind a piece of furniture and calls out to the one-year old. As the child approaches, the parent pops up with a "boo." On the other hand, "Hide and Seek" may be initiated by a toddler, who wanders off to play in a closet, only to find that Mom and Dad are calling for him all over the house.

In this chapter we look at several other characteristics of the physical games that parents share with their toddlers. We will see how parents can take ad-

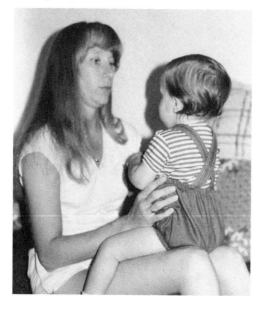

vantage of these characteristics to extend and elaborate old games, to introduce new play ideas, and to preserve the feelings of intimacy and togetherness that physical games elicit.

# A New Level of Vigor

Now that the children are walking well and rapidly developing new skills to accompany walking, physical games become more vigorous. By themselves the children may still be rather tentative and cautious but, with the support of parents, they are transformed into raring-to-go daredevils. In games of "peek-a-boo," for example, one-year olds enjoy staggering around the room with a blanket over their heads — bumping into walls and furniture, falling down — until finally the blanket is removed and they triumphantly emerge.

Lifting and swinging games, jumping routines, wrestling matches, all sorts of physical exchanges become rougher and more daring as toddlers grow. Many parents, for example, like to lie on their backs and lift one-year olds into the air with their feet. Balanced on their parents' feet, the children swing back and forth until they topple, usually head first into the arms of their parents. Children are regularly turned upside down as they dismount from a parent's shoulders or come down from a brief visit to the ceiling. No longer are "horsey rides" on Dad's leg limited to gentle"Old Nellies."When Dad sings, "Watch out — you're gonna get bucked off," he means it.

Gradually, one-year olds learn how to initiate these vigorous physical games. Spotting a parent who is resting on the floor, they are likely to sit on an unsuspecting stomach or head. A back that bends low enough to the ground is in danger of being pounced on; an outstretched leg encourages monkey bar antics. Parents who sit quietly minding their business become mountains over which to scramble. Each of these maneuvers by one-year olds can be opening moves in a physical game. In a manner that is well meaning but sometimes quite sudden, the children are asking parents: "Do you want to wake up and play with me?"

One of the best arenas for vigorous physical games is the playground. Parents and one-year olds can share equipment that would be too much for a child alone. Together they can zip down a tornado slide, get dizzy on a fast merry-go-round, ride a big tire swing, or operate a full-scale teeter totter. The children experience the thrill of danger while safely cradled in their parent's laps.

# A New Emphasis on Imagination

Just as one-year olds develop the strength and coordination for a new level of vigor, they develop the mental ability to understand imaginative twists to physical games. Parents naturally talk to their children while they play and, sooner or later, they make up story lines to go along with favorite physical games.

A game of "peek-a-boo," for example, fits the story line of going to sleep. "Night, night — sleep tight," the parent intones solemnly as the child is covered with a blanket. Then, as the child peeks out from under the cover, the parent acts amazed: "What? You're already awake? Okay, time to get up!" A few moments later, the parent renews the game. "Time to go to sleep."

Another common story line might be called "Anybody Home?" The child hides in the pantry and the parents pretend that they are visiting. They knock politely on the hideout door and inquire, "Anybody home?" There may be no answer until the parents carefully inch the door open, whereupon the one-year old occupant responds with a coy smile, a bubbling giggle, or a roar. "Oh, here's Miss Happy (or Mr. Gigglebox, or Pantry Monster)! the parents comment with surprise.

One of the most fertile imaginary themes in physical games is monster play. The imaginary monsters that ramble through the games between parents and one-year olds are, of course, quite benign. Frequently, the parent adopts a monster role in the context of a chase game. For months the parent has been chasing the child with the warning, "I'm gonna' get you!" Now the parent feels the need to follow through, to think of something more to do once the child has been "got." Monsters are usually hungry: the chase monster may love to nibble on the fingers, elbows, and ear lobes of a one-year old. Despite voracious chomping and growling noises, the child recognizes such attacks for what they are — barely disguised, but very slobbery, kisses. In time, the monster may promise to eat the whole child up, or graduate to some other extravagant threat:

> "I'm going to shake your brains out." (Obviously this requires holding the victim upside down.)
> "I'm going to send you flying to the moon." (This involves spinning around in a circle with the child held over your head.)
> "I'm going to throw you onto the trash heap." (A bean bag chair works well.) "And you'll *never, never* get down."

Any physical game that really catches on will also catch the imagination of parents and children. Suppose the child gets in the habit of jumping off the changing table into a parent's arms. Undoubtedly, the parent will give the child an imaginary identity. Perhaps it will be Superman coming out of the sky or Big Bird flying out of his nest. In the same way, a child who is continually being lifted into the air will probably assume a more suitable shape for flying, such as an airplane or a space shuttle. "5 . . . 4 . . . 3 . . . 2 . . . 1 . . . Blast Off!"

# The Teaching Potential of Physical Games

Adding an imaginative layer to physical games makes them more fun. It also floods a one year old's mind with new ideas. These ideas may be too exotic or mysterious to be understood right away, but they help children recognize the exciting potential of fantasy. Some physical games, on the other hand, are designed by parents to combine the fun of a game with teaching a child new words.

The most common game of this type focuses on learning names for different parts of the body. If the game for today is about noses, the child and parent may take turns squeezing each other's noses, or the child may go around the room touching the nose of every available player while the parent pronounces the word "nose" slowly and clearly. A body parts game can become still livelier if parents ease up on the direct instruction some of the time. They might quack or make some other unexpected noise when the toddler touches their nose. They might pretend the child has taken off the body part. "Hey, did you take my nose off? Well, put it back then."

The best physical games for teaching involve singing and dancing. Whether parents and one-year olds are exercising together, dancing to a record, or marching to the beat of their own home-made instruments, they can introduce new words and make them part of the game. Kenneth and his Dad were especially fond of the "Paddywhack" song. The sillier the rhymes that Dad could think up, the more fun they had with the game: "This old man, he said crummy; he played knick-knack on your tummy." (In other rhymes, smell-bow was used for elbow, squeeze for knees, and got-em for bottom.)

Jennifer and her mother played an animated version of "Here We Go 'Round the Mulberry Bush." Jennifer's mother began: "This is the way we clap our hands," as Jennifer did her best to follow the movements and hum along. Additional verses involved swinging their arms, kicking their feet and wiggling their bottoms. In a grand finale, Mother swept Jennifer off her feet and sang: "This is the way we fly to bed, fly to bed, fly to bed."

*     *     *

As children progress from one to two years of age, their repertoire of physical games with their parents is expanding. The games are becoming more complex in structure and involve a new level of vigor. They may include a new imaginary dimension or they may focus on teaching specific concepts. We have discussed physical games from these different perspectives, not to imply that parents ought to play in any particular way with their one-year olds, but to illuminate the different approaches that can be taken. Although a physical game may involve all of the characteristics we have discussed, many parents favor highlighting one perspective over another.

Physical games are expressions of intimacy, ways to extend hugging and kissing. Parents and one-year olds look for opportunities to touch each other, and touching leads spontaneously to a game. Suddenly, hands are joined in a "high five," or parent and child touch index fingers in the fashion of E.T. Spontaneity is the key ingredient in physical games, and the best games are those on which parents and children have put their personal mark. They are games that have grown out of the spirit of the moment, when both parents and children were open to new possibilities.

Let us describe a typical example, which we found when taking the pictures for this book. Michael and his mother had recently visited the zoo. Later, when Michael was playing in a favorite cupboard behind the couch, it seemed as though he was in a cage, too. Taking the cushions off the back of the couch created the illusion that Michael was actually in the zoo behind bars. He enjoyed making faces at his mother and kissing her through the bars. The game of "monkey in the zoo," begun during a moment of inspiration, delighted both Michael and his mother and soon became a featured attraction of their daily routine.

# Suggested Activities

## *Parts of the Body Games*

Toddlers like to learn the names for parts of their body. This learning is even more enjoyable when it comes in the form of a physical game. In this picture, a one-year old and his mother are playing a favorite game — touching index fingers and saying "E.T." Although no direct instruction is involved, the child will learn within the context of the game that he uses "fingers" to play E.T.

The well known song, "Where is Thumbkin?", can be adapted to fit any body part:

>   Where is elbow? (parent sings in tone of suspense)
>   Where is elbow?
>
>   Here it is! (suddenly grabbing child's elbow)
>   Here it is!
>
>   How are you today Sir? (Gently shaking, squeezing, or tickling elbow)

How are you today, Sir?
Are you fine?
Are you fine?

Many of these games involve a parent grabbing part of a toddler's body, or vice versa. A one-year old, for example, may start a game of grabbing Dad's glasses off his face. (Although glasses are not a part of the body, they seem so to a young child.) One way to redirect this playfulness is to suggest that the child grab your nose. Then you can provide a surprise by honking like a bus, growling like a dog, or grunting like a pig.

Another spontaneous game that may be difficult to manage occurs when your child tries to touch your eyes. Naturally you close your eyes, which only stimulates a toddler to try harder. You can substitute a game of "touch my tongue." The parent sticks out her tongue, then the child tries to touch it before it disappears back inside Mom's mouth.

Parts-of-the-body games are ways to express affection. A parent and toddler may slap their hands together in the fashion of "high five," rub noses, or join their toes in a wrestling match. Perhaps the most versatile game takes the form of "the hungry parent." The parent pretends to eat up special parts of the toddler's body: "Oh, a delicious ear — I think I'll nibble on this! Yum, yum, toes for dessert! . . . I'm still hungry — I'm going to eat up your neck!"

# Lifting and Wrestling Games

Toddlers love to be lifted high into the air and swung around. These games provide a natural way to teach words like "up and down," "around and around," and "Whew, am I tired." Here are two examples of lifting games.

A parent can lift the one-year old high enough to touch the ceiling. In this family, a game had evolved in which Dad walked around the house with his daughter on the ceiling. But each time he came to a doorway, he said "Whoops, she's stuck again." After rescuing her by lowering her through the door, back she went to the ceiling.

Another exciting form of lifting involves lying on your back and lifting your toddler with the bottom of your feet. "How do I get down from here?" your toddler may seem to be saying. With practice you will find a variety of ways to make the trip down as much fun as the trip up.

Wrestling is another way for parents and toddlers to play together vigorously. Some parents like to roll on the floor with a toddler, lifting their body as they roll on top of the child so that no weight is felt. Other parents kneel on the floor and put their head down, like a turtle inside his shell. One-year olds climb and jump on the "turtle shell" until suddenly, like a volcano erupting, the turtle rises and tosses the child this way and that. In the picture below, a parent is using a stuffed animal to wrestle. In this kind of wrestling match, the toddler is the one who is bigger and stronger.

## Hiding Games

Any version of hide and seek appeals to a toddler, as long as it is not difficult to find the person who is hiding. A blanket, whether on a bed or not, instantly creates a good hiding place. First the child hides in the blanket, then the parent takes a turn. It always is easy to recognize that big lump under the blanket.

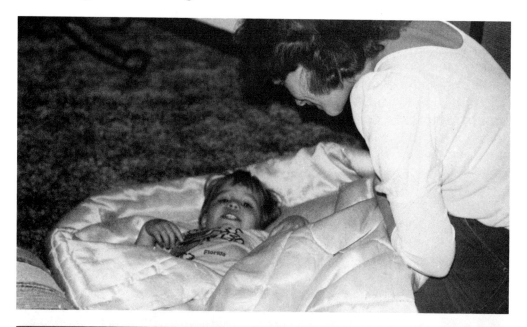

Hiding games are fun on a smaller scale as well. Now that your child understands the permanence of hidden objects, he will enjoy simple disappearing tricks." The penny is not in this hand, not in that hand, hmmm, here it is in your hair!" Objects can disappear, not very magically, into a child's sleeve or sock, or down the front of a child's shirt. One of the best "magic" tricks is to make something disappear into your pocket. Toddlers take great pleasure in foiling the magician and finding such objects.

# Chasing and Hugging Games

Parents love to chase toddlers and toddlers love to be chased. In fact, the object of the game is to be caught, for then the parent gives the toddler a big hug. The game can be extended by keeping toddlers in friendly custody, thereby challenging them to escape again. A parent might trap the child between his legs, hold the child by one foot, or pretend to sit on the child.

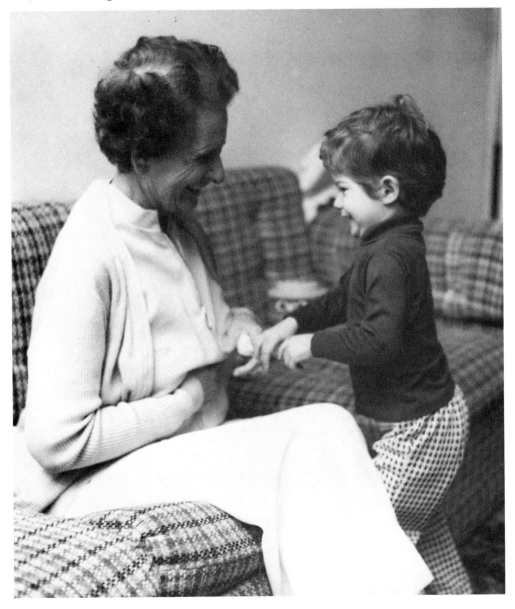

## Sound Games

Many physical games involve making playful sounds. Sooner or later, parents and toddlers discover that all sorts of sounds, including whispers and normal speech, are more intriguing when broadcast through a cardboard tube. The longer the tube, the more amazing the phenomenon. The sound, whatever it is, comes from the end of the tube instead of a person's mouth.

# Chapter 10
# PLAYING WITH TOYS

| The Scene: | A telephone conversation. |
|---|---|
| Grandma: | "What would you like me to buy for Anthony? I know he already has a million toys. I thought maybe he could use a new jacket or a nice warm sweater." |
| Mother: | "Just bring yourself—we can't wait...." |
| Grandma: | "Now you know I'm not coming empty-handed so you might as well tell me what he needs." |
| Mother: | "Well, to tell the truth, he has plenty of clothes but he's outgrowing his baby toys. He just loves balls and trucks and, you know what else? He's ready for some simple puzzles." |

Like Anthony's mother, parents of one to two-year olds get almost as much pleasure out of a new toy as their children do. A new toy not only keeps a toddler busy and happy, it also offers fresh possibilities for parent-child play. Parents love to help their toddler complete a new puzzle, or put a train set together. A carefully selected toy gives parents an opportunity to help toddlers learn new concepts and share in their feelings of mastery.

In this chapter, we focus on the way parents and one-year olds play with a variety of toys. In particular, we look at ball play, building with blocks, playing with cars and trucks, and pretend play with dolls. With each kind of play, we discuss how parents can help their children develop new skills. Throughout the chapter, we stress the importance of letting children practice familiar games, invent new games on their own, and make their own discoveries.

# Playing With a Ball

A ball is probably the single most popular toy for one-year olds, for parents, or for any age. Balls do two of the most curious things: they bounce and they roll. One-year olds realize that most objects fall directly to the ground when released. Balls, however, don't follow the rule. Instead of staying on the ground, they bounce back up, and instead of coming to rest where they are dropped, they roll off in any direction.

Because balls are so unpredictable when they bounce and roll, ball play is a natural for two people. A toddler version of fetch is a good beginning ball game. The adult throws the ball and the child chases it down and brings it back. A large ball, like a basketball, is easy to track down, and carrying it back to the parent is a challenge in itself. Another early version of ball play involves the toddler tossing the ball to the adult from up close. The adult

catches the ball and then hands it back to the child for another round of target practice. A good ball for this kind of one-sided catch is a small ball that the child can grasp easily, such as a miniature football.

Some time between the ages of one and two, most children become interested in a true game of catch. The idea of sending a ball back and forth between two players, as pointless as it really is, makes sense to a toddler. Still, there is the problem of keeping the ball in bounds. The simplest way to manage this problem is for the parent and child to sit facing each other with

their legs spread out. They can roll the ball back and forth and be reasonably certain that the ball will be trapped by their outstretched legs, unless of course it dies between them from lack of steam. A more vigorous game of catch can be kept in bounds by playing in a hallway. The ball may get beyond one of the players but the walls of the hallway block deviant throws to the right or left. A ball court for a really wild game of catch is a staircase. The child can stand on the landing (with one parent nearby to keep the child from falling) while the other parent stands at the bottom of the stairs. Any kind of throw will reach the bottom of the stairs, where the parent retrieves the ball and pitches it back up.

Parents may be concerned that this ball play will prove destructive. There is no denying that an uninhibited game of catch inside the house can break something. Toy manufacturers have dealt effectively with this problem by producing nerf balls. Parents who want to restrict indoor ball play can introduce other non-destructive balls as well. A ping-pong ball is harmless but versatile. It can be thrown with ease but will not sail very far because it is so light. It is not likely to hurt anything it hits, and yet it has the lively bounce of a hard ball. Another possibility is to make balls out of newspaper. Although the balls are not much like real balls (no bounce, no roll), it is fun to squash and mold the newspaper and then throw it into a receptacle. This is the well-known basketball game practiced in offices throughout the country. What these balls lack in quality, they make up in quantity, for a single day's newspaper provides enough material for a whole basketful of balls.

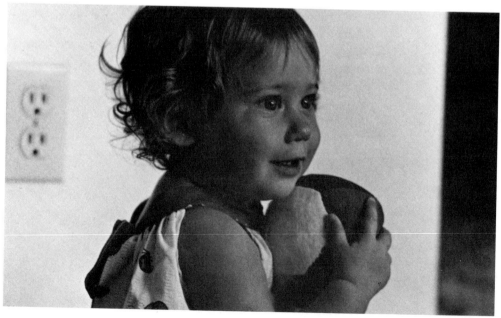

Catching a ball is more difficult than throwing one and toddlers, for the most part, are not very good at it. Typically, a toddler will stand with his arms out while the ball bounces against his tummy. Parents who are interested in teaching their children to catch are best off starting with a balloon or a large beach ball. Eventually many parents become interested in teaching their children other kinds of ball games. They help their children learn to hit a ball with a baseball bat, a golf club, or a tennis racquet. For the time being, however, one-year olds have their hands full just exploring the surprising assortment of balls that exist, from the incredible bounciness of a racquet ball to the slippery heaviness of a bowling ball.

# Playing With Blocks and Building Materials

In an earlier chapter we talked about how children are interested in emptying things before they turn their attention to filling. We see this same sort of progression in block play. Long before toddlers show a spontaneous interest in building block towers, they obviously relish knocking them down. Actually, the game of "build and crash" that children play with parents is an early experiment in balance. In this game, children recognize the instability of their parent's tower and take on the mischievous role of upsetting the balance. In other spontaneous games, which are not on so grand a scale, toddlers may take over the role of the balancer. A miniature cow is stood up on its legs or a doll is balanced on the window sill.

Balance experiments with one-year olds can be extended in at least two ways. For children who show an inclination to build higher, parents can demonstrate how a tower may be constructed in layers. Each layer consists of a pedestal with objects balanced on top of it. Large flat books and cookie sheets work well as the pedestals, while blocks or margarine containers are placed between the layers. The same idea can work with large hard books and small tin cans: place several cans on top of the book, then another book across the cans, more cans on top and another book, etc. The tower looks like a Dagwood sandwich, with books for slices of bread and tin cans as the fixings.

The second kind of extension occurs when one-year olds become interested in arranging a set of objects on top of a pedestal. One miniature doll on the arm of a chair is joined by the rest of the doll family, or one hot-wheels car parked on top of a tomato juice can is transformed into a parking lot full of cars.

As toddlers get interested in crowding a collection of objects onto a ped-

estal, they are exploring the possibility of building on a horizontal plane. Some toddlers are intrigued with the idea of horizontal building and will make long lines with all sorts of things: playing cards, blocks, magazines, or the shoes from everyone's closet. Parents can capitalize on this new interest by introducing new materials or suggesting new combinations. The line of magazines can become a highway for toy cars, a farm animal can be placed on top of each playing card to create a miniature farm. These elaborations make building activities come alive and foster the child's beginning interest in pretending.

# Playing With Cars and Trucks

Cars and trucks of all sizes and varieties are among the most popular items in every toy store. The fascination with cars and trucks begins at a very early age. One of the most popular toys on the market is a child-size car with a door that opens and closes and a steering wheel that turns. As a toddler steps into a real-looking car, shuts the door, turns the key, and twirls the steering wheel, his intense expression tells us that, at least for the moment, he is in the driver's seat.

Although toddlers enjoy big vehicles they can scoot on, or steering wheels they can maneuver, miniature vehicles offer the greatest possibilities for parent-child play. Games with miniature vehicles emerge spontaneously as

toddlers and parents push their vehicles along the floor, making "vrum vrum" noises. Sometimes these games are quite simple. Parents and toddlers drive their cars around the room, under the table or along the edge of the sofa. Perhaps they experiment with a somewhat rougher terrain and drive their cars over each others' bodies. Maneuvering up a leg, across a stomach, around a neck and through a head of hair proves to be a ticklish trip. The road twitches and wiggles as it is traversed. A driving fame such as "Hide and Seek," may be played, with the parent driving in a circle around the child, now behind the child's back, now in front, bumping over the child's toes, or shooting between the child's legs.

Another variation of car play is "Follow the Leader." "Come on, follow me," the parent can say to start the game. Then, as the parent drives in and around pieces of furniture and the child follows, the parent provides a running commentary: "Okay, up the table leg...Up (unh), up (unh)..shift into low gear (rrhhRRR)...Now around the sugar bowl...no stopping for food...Jump off the side (Yahhhh)!"

For parents and children interested in building, cars and trucks provide an obvious extension of block play. Blocks can be used to build simple garages or parking lots for favorite cars. Parents can help their one-year olds build short tunnels to drive cars through, or bridges over which the cars can drive. Ramps and hills can be created with blocks or plastic trays.

As your child becomes better able to understand imaginary play, you may want to introduce more elaborate themes related to vehicles. One theme might be called "taking care of the car." Toddlers notice that cars are constantly in need of more gas, more air, or some other kind of maintenance. Phillip, at eighteen months, was especially intrigued with drive-through car washes, and so it was quite natural for Phillip and his father to go into the car-wash business. Using a cut-up shoebox, they created a tunnel for washing their collection of miniature vehicles. Systematically, Phillip gave each car a turn driving through the car wash. His father maintained a pitch of excitement by taking on the role of announcer. "Here comes Phillip driving the Chevrolet! Up to the car wash he comes! Swish-swish-swish. On goes the water— Here come the soap suds—Off goes the water—Out comes the car!"

Children like Phillip who have a strong interest in real vehicles may respond to a variety of imaginary themes if stimulated by their parents. However, these pretend episodes with a one-year old will usually remain very brief. Most of the time one-year olds and their parents just tune into the movement of their toy vehicles. They are caught up in the way the rolling motion of the wheels is transferred to the hand of the would-be driver, the feel of the open road in a driving fantasy.

# Playing With Dolls

Whether a rag doll wears a face that is happy or sad, one's first impulse is to give it some love. The doll's big button eyes and stitched-on mouth bring out one's protective feelings. Parents naturally communicate this attitude to their one-year olds. Seeing a doll on the floor, they urge their one-year old to pick it up and give it a reassuring hug.

Indeed, parents can encourage their one-year olds to respond in a variety of ways to the presumed unhappiness of dolls and stuffed animals. A doll may be crying because it is hungry and needs to be fed, or because it is tired and wants to go to bed. Perhaps the crying means the doll is cold and should be wrapped in a blanket. Maybe the doll is simply upset and needs to be rocked in a rocking chair. Naturally these various responses to imag-

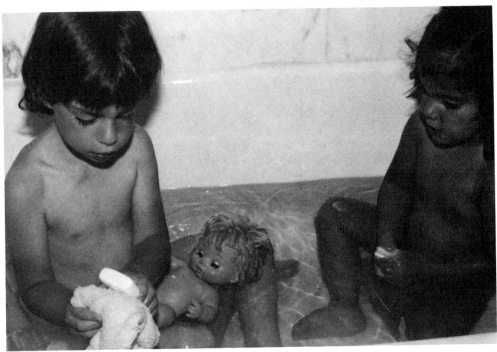

ined distress are first modeled by parents (or older children), and then gradually adopted by one-year olds.

Parents who choose to elaborate on the unhappiness of dolls and stuffed animals do so because they enjoy caregiving play with their children. These parents are oriented toward stimulating a child's sense of empathy, and they feel good when they see their one-year olds pretending to be helpful and caring. The children may not be learning much about real caregiving, but they are picking up through play the importance of empathizing with another person's discomfort.

Projecting aches and pains on a doll is only the starting point for encouraging nurturance. Parents who want to realize the potential of doll play can invest a doll or stuffed animal with positive feelings as well. Speaking for the doll, the parents can bring out these feelings. "Hi," a doll may greet the one-year old in the morning. "Do you want to see me dance?" "Let's go take a bath," a doll may suggest, "I want to splash water." Dolls that converse, instead of just crying, become friends and companions, giving the one-year old a chance to empathize with a wider range of emotions.

Over time, each doll and stuffed animal which is animated by parents acquires a unique personality. A large blue dragon becomes known as the "tickling dragon" because he specializes in wrestling with a one-year old. A fat bear who is perpetually hungry joins the child at breakfast time. A doll with gymnastic tendencies regularly asks the child to catch her as she goes down the slide or jumps into the crib. This cast of characters enables parents to speak to their toddler in several voices, to offer adult guidance and

suggestions in a variety of playful guises. More importantly, the child is surrounded by a group of friends. It is as if the charm of the "Sesame Street" Muppets has been drawn out of the television set and into the child's home.

Parents who encourage doll play find it has practical advantages too. Acting out a simplified sleep routine with a stuffed animal helps a one-year old accept bedtime. Giving a baby doll a bottle of water instead of milk makes it easier for the one-year old to accept a similar substitution. In time, doll play may even provide a way for one-year olds to reassure themselves. Children who get in the habit of rocking an upset doll or putting a doll to sleep may use these play routines to comfort themselves.

Parents can lay the groundwork for independent doll play by using simple props in their demonstrations. A receiving blanket for the doll's clothes, a cardboard box for a bed, a doll bottle for feeding, these are adequate accessories in the beginning. They are simple enough to be used by one-year olds without adult assistance, when and if the children act out imaginary themes on their own.

Ultimately the success of doll play depends upon children forming attachments to their dolls. Parents can point out that dolls are crying and they can give them personalities, but they cannot determine a child's feeling toward the dolls. A one-year old may prefer stuffed animals to traditional dolls. A collection of miniature characters who can travel together in a bucket or bag may be adopted by the child. Imaginary babies and friends come in many forms, and children do not always select the ones that parents find most attractive.

In fact, when one-year olds first start playing with dolls, their favorites often become distinctly less attractive. Out of curiosity, the children pull off or poke out the doll's eyes. They twist off arms, legs and heads. Parents can anticipate this mutilation and respond by fixing the dolls as much as possible in a kindly, matter-of-fact way. The children's behavior does not foreshadow a cruel nature. Quite likely, by the time they are approaching the age of two, these same children will show special concern for the doll who is missing an eye or who has lost most of its hair.

Within the broad themes of caregiver-play and friendship-play, there are many different ways to pretend with dolls and stuffed animals. Parents can concentrate on games that appeal to them. Some doll characters may even seem like members of the family. Their presence will be sporadic, however, for parents cannot act as the eyes and ears of the dolls all the time. When parents do have time to play, they are teaching their children the fundamental idea of pretending: life can be attributed to lifeless objects. It is exciting for parents to see this idea dawning in the minds of one-year olds as they talk to their dolls and stuffed animals.

# Suggested Activities

## Playing With Balls

One of the earliest ways to play with a ball is a game of "fetch." The parent rolls a ball across the floor and the toddler retrieves it. If your child is walking well, a basketball is ideal for this game because it is such a challenge to pick up and carry.

As your child progresses to a game of catch, you will notice that his ability to throw far exceeds his ability to catch. You can solve this problem by handing your child a small ball, encouraging him to throw it to you, and then handing it back to him for another throw. This means that you and your child will be only three to five feet apart, which is just about the right range for a one-year old's throwing skill.

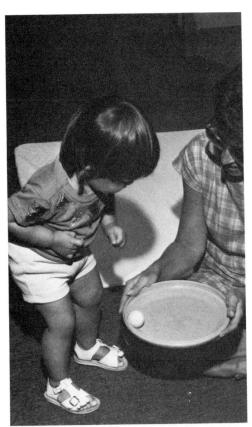

Inside ball games can be nerve-racking. However, there are a variety of balls that are satisfactory. In this picture, a one-year old is playing with a paper ball. Other "safe" balls include a ping-pong ball, nerf balls, rolled up socks, and a ball of yarn.

If your child is interested in learning to catch a ball, a balloon or beach ball works best. It moves slowly enough to be tracked and is relatively easy to trap against the chest. Of course, blowing up the ball is half the fun.

Golf and tennis balls are not very suitable for indoor play, but their bounciness is intriguing. Dropping a golf ball on a driveway and then trying to chase it down, is a game with endless variations for a toddler. Here a parent is playing an indoor game with the same kind of unpredictability. As the pan is tilted, the golf ball rolls back and forth around the outer edge—just slow enough to look like it can be caught by the child, just fast enough to be one step ahead of her outstretched hand.

# Playing With Blocks and Building Materials

When toddlers first show interest in tower building, they are most impressed with their ability to knock down towers. You can encourage your child to experiment with building towers by showing him how to balance a miniature doll or animal on top of the tower. As a lookout, the tower is likely to be left standing a little bit longer.

Many toddlers are interested in stacking household objects. Tin cans, toilet paper rolls, or margarine tubs may be preferred as building materials. Tin cans are very stable, especially full cans, although you may worry that they are too heavy for the child to handle safely. Empty tin cans can be made more appealing by decorating them with wrapping paper or wallpaper scraps.

More complex towers can be built in layers. First a short tower is built and topped with a horizontal support, such as a book or cookie sheet. Then additional layers can be constructed in the same way. This advanced kind of tower is good for parents who enjoy building with their one-year olds.

It is easier to build flat constructions because the problem of balance does not need to be solved. Given a variety of interesting shapes and colors, your child may be interested in creating a design or enclosure. At first toddlers tend to combine only a few pieces, perhaps repeating their discovery a number of times. Gradually their ideas become more expansive. You may want to make an occasional suggestion, but this is a good opportunity for you to observe your child's awareness and interest in spatial relationships.

One-year olds who like building usually explore the nature of a straight line. They may line up toy cars, animals, balls, virtually anything. You can introduce a game of "fill the hole." Make a line with a set of objects, then move an object from the middle of the line to one end: "I think I'll move up here—chug-chug-chug." Wait to see if your child does anything to fill this hole in the middle of the line. If not, demonstrate a possible solution by moving a second object into the first hole. This creates a second hole. As you and your child fill old holes and make new ones, you will be putting together and taking apart the line. It is like building up and knocking down a tower, except that the line is not destroyed everytime a hole is created in it.

# *Playing With Cars and Trucks*

The most exciting terrain for driving toy cars is another person's body. You and your toddler can have a lot of fun exploring the highways and byways created by the different parts of the human body. As you drive there will be many opportunities to acquaint your child with words like "up, down, in, out, over, through, or under."

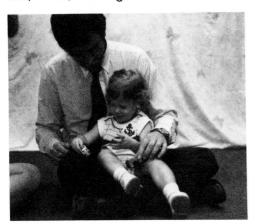

Another good surface for driving is the dining or kitchen table. You and your toddler can maneuver your cars without crawling on the floor. Try a game of "Follow-the-Leader." Encourage your child to follow your lead as you perform various stunts: driving around a plate, jumping the salt shaker, and hiding under a napkin.

Playing with cars and trucks is more fun when you add some simple block structures. You can build a tunnel for cars to go through, a garage for parking, or a ramp for racing. In fact, all kinds of building stuff offers possibilities. Cars can be pushed through cardboard tubes, balanced on top of margarine containers, and raced down cookie sheet ramps.

If you like to play with cars and trucks, you can introduce some pretend themes that will be novel for your one-year old. One possibility is to pretend you are fixing the cars, putting gasoline in them, or washing them. Another possibility is to pretend you are taking a trip in a car or truck. A third idea is to use a toy dumptruck for deliveries. The truck might deliver popcorn, for example, to members of the family while they are watching television. Perhaps dirty socks might be transported to the clothes hamper.

## Playing With Dolls

Now that your toddler has learned to give hugs, he or she will enjoy giving love to a doll or stuffed animal. Holding a doll close seems to be the first and most basic step toward becoming that doll's caregiver.

Another basic step in becoming a caregiver is to begin feeding a doll or stuffed animal. Toddlers like for parents to join them in this new form of doll play. Here, a one year old girl pretends to feed her doll some cheerios. After holding each cheerio to the doll's mouth, she naturally eats it herself.

Not all toddlers are attracted to doll play. If your child is, you will find that simple props can stimulate independent play. A blanket, for example, works well for dressing the baby, a cardboard box makes a good crib, and a plastic baby bottle suffices for feeding. More elaborate props are not necessary and they may cause frustration.

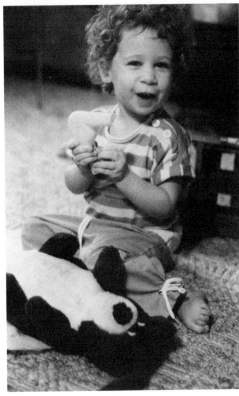

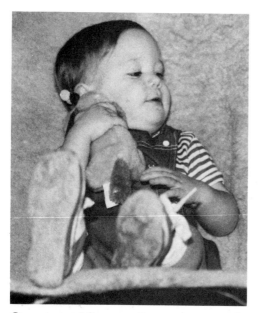

One-year olds sometimes want to play out more advanced themes with their dolls. In this picture, a toddler is pretending to dry his dog's hair with the hair dryer. Any experience with strong emotional significance may be re-enacted in doll play, especially if you participate in the play.

Dolls usually start out as babies, but soon they become peer friends as well. Your one-year old may enjoy sharing a variety of experiences with this new friend. Together they may go down the slide, ride on the back of a bicycle, or take a bath in the tub.

Dolls are very exciting companions when they talk. You can become the voice of a favorite doll or stuffed animal. Whether or not your one-year old is talking much, the chance to interact with an animated doll will be seen as a special treat.

Many toddlers are attracted to miniature dolls. If your child likes to carry around several of these dolls, introduce a game of "taking turns." The dolls might be "jumping" off the window ledge or riding in a toy bus. Whatever they are doing, there will be an opportunity for you to demonstrate the idea of taking turns: "Okay, Bert. Now it's your turn to jump. Good! Now, Ernie, it's your turn...Everybody will get a chance."

## Chapter 11
# LEARNING THROUGH LANGUAGE

| | |
|---|---|
| The Scene: | Rachel, age twenty-one months, is at the playground with her mother. Phillip, a three-year old, arrives just as Rachel comes down the slide. |
| Rachel: | (Giving Phillip an ineffective push.) "My slide." |
| Rachel's Mother: | (Holding her squirming daughter around the waist.) "It's Phillip's turn, Rachel. Watch Phillip. Good sliding, Phillip. Now it's Rachel's turn." |
| Rachel: | (After scurrying up and down the slide.) "Now Phillip's turn." |

When toddlers first learn to communicate ideas through language, words have a special fascination. Rachel was delighted with learning the words, "my turn." Sharing the slide with Phillip was perfectly acceptable when it gave her an opportunity to practice her new words.

Learning to communicate with words is unquestionably a major accomplishment of the early childhood years. Because the development of language is such an amazing feat, it is natural for parents to pay close attention to their child's progress. Every new word their toddler uses becomes a source of delight. At the same time, if a toddler is talking less then other children they know, parents are likely to feel anxious.

Toddlers learn language at different times, at different rates and in different ways. Some toddlers talk in two word phrases by the time they are fourteen months old. Other toddlers who are also developing normally may be saying only a few words at the age of two. Some toddlers seem to burst into language, some learn in fits and starts, while others acquire new words at a slow and steady rate. As long as children are responsive to the language they hear, and enjoy making word-like sounds, parents can be sure that their child will speak in due course.

Because all children have a spontaneous interest in learning language, parents can capitalize on this interest in their role as language teachers. Rather than quizzing their children every minute, "Say 'Mommy,' say 'Nana,' What does a doggie say?" parents can talk to their child in a casual way about everyday things. They can expand on their child's comments, speak in short sentences, and include their child in a give and take conversation.

| | |
|---|---|
| Toddler: | "Ball." |
| Parent: | (Looking in the toy box.) "Yes, your ball is in the toy box." |
| Toddler: | "Uh-uh." |
| Parent: | "Oh, your ball is stuck in the box. Do you want me to take it out?" |

Even if the toddler's contribution to the conversation is only an interested stare, the free and easy prattle of the parent is an impetus to language acquisition.

Once children begin the process of learning language, they may expand their language repertoire in several ways. Some children tend to be name-callers. Before putting words together, they learn the names of all the things and people they know. Other children are "phrase catchers." They learn three or four useful phrases and then put them to use in many different situations.

Nicholas was essentially a "name-calling" child. At a very young age, he learned to call the car, "Vrum-vrum," his food, "Yum," and his favorite teddy bear, "bah." In his first language expansion, he experimented with using these words in different contexts: "Vrum-vrum" was used to say, 'I want to go for a ride in the car," "I hear Daddy's car in the driveway," or "I see a picture of a car on the back cover of a magazine." After a while, Nicholas took on the task of expanding his own vocabulary. As he read through a book with his mother, he would place his finger on something on the page and look up at his mother expectantly. His mother would obligingly give the picture a name which Nicholas would repeat. By about twenty-months, Nicho-

las could attach a name to everything he saw. Only then did Nicholas turn his attention to the task of combining words.

Rachel, who was the youngest in a family of three, had a very different pattern of language acquisition. With the exception of the people in her environment, Rachel showed little interest in naming things. She wanted to talk like her siblings. Not surprisingly, Rachel mastered several phrases at an early age which she used in a variety of contexts. "I want it," "Don't like that," and "That mine," were her first well-practiced phrases. Finally, when she needed to be more explicit about her needs, Rachel added new words to her vocabulary. "I want juice, I want milk, I want my dolly."

Although children acquire language at different rates and through different routes, some time between the ages of eighteen months and three years most children will have mastered the fundamentals of language. At whatever time it occurs, sharing the discovery of language is one of the purest delights of parenting a toddler.

# Reading Books With Children

Mother:   (Opening the door for her husband.) "Oh, am I glad you're home early tonight. This son of yours has been a holy terror. Here he is, he heard you coming." (At this point Andrew, age 15 months, falls into his father's arms.)

Andrew:   "Dadda car. Dadda car."

Father: (Kissing Andrew and then placing him back on the floor.) "No, young man, we are not going for a car ride. Besides, Mommy tells me that you've been a holy terror. So what did you do today?"

Mother: (Still a bit hassled.) "Andrew pulled the leaves off the new philodendron plant, scribbled on the telephone bill, and stuffed the bathroom towels into the toilet."

Father: "Sounds like it's time for a serious father and son talk. How come you're giving your mother such a hard time?" (Father walks into the family room and sits on a large chair.)

Andrew: (Walking toward his father with a book in his hand) "Up, Dadda. Up."

Father: "So you want to make up, do you?" Hmm, let's see. *Pat the Bunny.* Aren't you a little young for this risqué kind of stuff?"

Mother: (Smiling broadly.) "Looks like you two will be busy for a while. I'll go and get dinner."

When a toddler climbs up on our lap with a book in hand, mischievous antics and negative moments are immediately forgotten. All parents are quite naturally delighted with their toddler's fascination with books. Book reading combines opportunities for intimacy and cuddling with opportunities to teach. It has none of the negatives associated with many other toddler activities. It is not noisy, wasteful, or destructive, and it doesn't make a mess. Best of all, a toddler's absorption in a reading activity carries with it the promise of future scholarly interests.

Despite parental preferences, toddlers' fascination with books is neither universal nor constant. Some toddlers will have nothing to do with books at all. Others go through phases. One week they are almost fanatical about wanting a parent to read to them. The next week they wriggle out of their parents' laps and fling the book across the room. Obviously, when toddlers are going through an "I hate reading" phase, trying to force them to read is counterproductive. However, parents can try to stimulate and prolong book-loving phases. Here are some strategies that were suggested by the families we visited.

"In our family, we sit down after dinner and spend about a half hour reading. I have two small rocking chairs, one for my three-year old and one for the baby. I put a pile of books on the floor beside each of the rocking chairs. For a while, Terry and Susie (Susie is 18 months old) sit in their own rocking

chairs and turn the pages of a book. Then both children climb up on my lap, and I help them read a story. It's a happy time of day. Of course, I guess it wouldn't work as well if we had three children instead of two."

"Michael was turned off from reading books for a long time. Then I started getting him interested in looking at pictures. I pointed out the family photos on the wall, posters in the store windows, the emblems on his T-shirts, the pictures in magazines - even the baby on the diaper box. I don't know if it's just coincidence, but he's back to loving books.

"Most of the time, Kathleen is too busy to sit down and read a book, but what she really enjoys is a matching game. I find the car in her book, and she runs to get her toy car. We do the same thing with a brush, doll, shoes and spoon. I am hoping that after a while she will get interested in just looking at the pictures and naming the things she sees."

## Selecting Appropriate Books

Once a toddler has become interested in "reading," the choice of books becomes important. Books that receive a stamp of approval from both toddlers and parents usually meet the following criteria:

—Illustrations that are bright, distinct, attractive, and not overly stylized.
—Illustrations that lend themselves to a game of hide and seek, that is, small familiar objects repeated on several pages.
—Illustrations that invite sound effects and encourage toddlers to participate. (The cow says "Moo," or the horn goes "Beep-Beep.")
—Stories that are about familiar objects such as animals, food, cars, and things around the house.
—Stories that describe everyday wants and daily routines. (In this category, an all-time favorite is *Goodnight Moon*.)
—Stories about "calamities," such as making a mess, breaking something, or getting very dirty. (These are especially appreciated by older toddlers.)
—Books that can be manipulated, such as 'touch-me' books like *Pat the Bunny*, 'dress-up' books with zippers and snaps, 'scratch and sniff' books, 'squeeze and squeak' books, books with tabs that make something happen, and books with stick-on characters. (Three dimensional pop-up books intrigue toddlers, but don't work very well because the toddler damages them.)
—Books that are sturdy, with pages that are easy to turn.

Naturally, all these characteristics are not always found in the same book. Parents need to "stock up" on the kinds of books that their own toddler enjoys most, but have other books available for variety. Some books, like some foods, can be introduced more slowly.

# Ways of Reading to Young Children

Reading a book to a toddler requires a parent's undivided attention. The sense of intimacy and togetherness that goes along with reading a book is destroyed when the parent has to answer the telephone, turn off the stove, or respond to the needs of other household members. Although uninterrupted time is a scarce commodity in most homes, parents can try to set aside regular times to read books with their one-year olds. Once the habit is established, parents report that this reading interlude is a relaxing and pleasant time of the day.

Being a proficient reader is not really important when it comes to reading to a toddler. As a matter of fact, the most effective readers tend to ignore the printed words altogether. Children are interested in pictures and it is up to parents to interpret the pictures in a way that the child understands. For the young toddler who is in the beginning stages of listening to a story, reading a book is like playing a game of "peek-a-boo." The toddler wants to turn the pages by himself, one at a time, forwards or backwards. Then the child closes and opens the book to see the same picture again.

When a toddler wants to read a book peek-a-boo style, the best strategy for the parent is simply to label the pictures. After a while the child may be ready to engage in a game of "Hide and Seek." "Now where's the teddy bear?" the parent may ask. "Where is the kitty who's going night-night?"

With most toddlers, "Hide and Seek reading" eventually leads to more active labeling. Now the children point to the pictures and proudly provide the labels themselves. At times, parents may use humor as a way of refueling their children. If a child has nothing to say about a page, the parent might mislabel a familiar object. "I see a mouse," Daddy declares as he points to a picture of a cow. "That's a moo-moo," the child insists, giggling at Daddy's silly error. The parent goes on, "Oh, yea! That's a moo-moo. The moo-moo is eating an ice cream cone."

These labeling games may continue to be prominent, off and on, for several years as children learn the names of unusual vehicles and exotic animals. Books that are designed for labeling, such as Richard Scary's word books, enable young children to label many objects that they have not seen (and may never see) in real life. They also help children see more in the real environment. Having learned a new word like "bridge" from a book, a one-year old may begin to see and point out real bridges.

As toddlers get older and become more proficient at understanding language, parents automatically change their way of reading. The labeling

strategy is abandoned, and parents almost instinctively start paraphrasing the story by describing what is happening in the pictures. In the process, they help their children make connections between one page and another. A story about a sleeping kitty might sound like this:

> "The kitty is asleep in the basket. Sh-sh, we have to be quiet, we don't want the kitty to wake up. Oh look, there's a little boy. Look, he has a drum just like your drum! Bang, bang, bang, he's making lots of noise. Oh, poor kitty. She's not sleeping any more. She's not in her basket. Kitty is all gone. Let's look for the kitty, That's right - turn the page. Good for you, you found the kitty! The kitty is under the chair."

Although children's books are the most common prop for labeling and storytelling, there are many quite reliable substitutes. Any kind of magazine, catalogue, or collection of greeting cards can serve as the basis of a reading experience. Of all the home-made books, the best and certainly the most popular is the family photo album. Many babies, even before they are one year old, recognize the entire family, including the cat and dog. And as the toddlers become more adept with language, they are able to identify events as well as people. The pleasure of a picnic at the beach, or a trip to the zoo can be repeated over and over through a photo sequence.

## Teaching Your Toddler to Read

Many toddlers who have become avid book "readers" develop the surprising talent of identifying their books by the cover. Recognizing the fact that these children have an extraordinary memory for visual images, some parents are sold on the idea of teaching their toddler to read. Using a 'sight-say' approach, they write familiar words in large letters on flash cards. Despite the enthusiasm of parent-teachers, toddlers do not readily learn a large vocabulary of sight words. With practice they will recognize a few dozen words, but being able to associate an isolated word with a flashcard is an insignificant part of reading. True reading involves comprehending the collective meaning of words that are organized into sentences and paragraphs. For a one-year old, the best preparation for reading is the development of basic listening and speaking skills. These skills will help the child learn more about how meaning is built into language and, at the same time, provide a high level of new information for the child to process.

Simply stated, reading a word like "cat" is not an important accomplishment. What is important is talking about all the interesting characteristics of cats. And books are an excellent resource for this kind of conversation.

Recognizing the present pleasures and future benefits that come from reading to a one-year old, it is not surprising that parents look upon books as one of their child's most valuable toys. By selecting appropriate books, by arranging for special reading time, and by making each reading session a comfortable and happy experience, parents can create the foundation for a life-long love of books.

# Conversational Play

| The Scene: | A child-sized table with a play tea set on it. |
|---|---|
| Theresa: | "Sit down Daddy, chair." |
| Father: | "Oh, dinner must be ready. And what did you make for dinner tonight?" |
| Theresa: | "Want psghetti, Daddy?" |
| Father: | "Psghetti - exactly what I want for dinner tonight." (Father puts the empty plastic fork to his mouth and makes a face.) "It's too hot." |
| Theresa: | "I blow it for you." |
| Father: | "That's better. MMMMM! I think it needs a little pinch of garlic." |
| Theresa: | "Here some pink garlic. Eat it all up. Don't pill it, Daddy." |

Many children start pretending to eat and drink when they are young toddlers. This pretending begins as imitation and is carried out with actions rather than words. As children approach the age of two, their growing language skills open the door to scenarios that are increasingly conversational. The highlight of a tea party is not simply pretending to drink from the cup but imagining what it contains. "Do you want to drink lemonade or chocolate milk?" the parent may wonder. "Drink coffee," the child replies decisively. In the same way, the imaginary cookies are more than just opportunities for chewing; they are topics of conversation. The child is delighted when parents comment about a cookie being burned or needing a little extra sugar.

New toys, as well as new ways to use old toys, become prominent in these conversational games. In the case of pretend eating, children become in-

terested in play dishes which formalize the activity and stimulate conversation. Having a plate leads to talking about what is on it. As the process of eating is further extended to include preparing and cooking food, the children enjoy using toy pots and pans and a toy stove. Naturally these first forays into cooking are limited. Like any novice cook, the children keep serving the same dishes again and again: soup, eggs, brownies. But even a limited menu offers many possibilities for parent-child conversation. A particularly good spot for this early cooking is the bathtub, assuming parents do not object to an occasional sip of bath water. There is a ready supply of cooking ingredients and spills are no problem.

Another new play theme rich in conversational possibilities is "going bye-bye." The most likely version is a shopping trip. For some time the children have been interested in pushing a toy shopping cart or a stroller around the house. They also, from time to time, have tried on bits of adult apparel: a necklace, a pair of shoes, a hat. Now they may be putting these two routines together in a sensible way. They get dressed up in adult garb in order to go shopping. Although the children look ready to go, they probably do not have a clear idea why they are shopping or even where they are going. Conversation with a parent will clarify matters, lengthen the play, and make it more fun. The parent can suggest a logical shopping place, "Are you going to Safeway?" or give a simple order, "Get me some pickles, please." The parent can hand the child a few coins to "spend" at the store, or offer a tongue-in-cheek piece of gratuitous advice, "Be careful crossing the streets."

Left on their own, one-year olds don't usually follow through and fill the shopping cart. Parents, if they wish, can accompany the children through the house and help them fill up the cart. Then they can proceed to the child's room in order to put the purchases away. A shopping trip benefits from this kind of closure; it makes the whole effort seem worthwhile. An alternative is for parents to play the part of the storekeeper, offering to sell various items of merchandise to their children. Of course, it is more like giving them the merchandise because one-year olds do not understand the reciprocal nature of buying and selling. They do enjoy moving coins or other tokens in and out of a cash register. A register that is easy to operate is a good toy to buy for a child interested in shopping.

The "bye-bye" theme may appear in the form of going to work. The child sits on a riding toy, waves goodbye, and wheels out of the room. Again, parents can elaborate the play with their comments, wishing the child a good day and reminding the child to return home for supper. The parents might suggest an accessory such as a lunchbox, a notebook, wallet, or sunglasses. Although outings to the beach, the park, or the mountains are relatively uncommon, older toddlers may collect a towel as if going swimming or show interest in a picnic cooler. Parents can respond by pretending that the children are going on a trip.

A familiar toy with obvious potential for conversational games is the telephone. In the living room, a parent and one-year old may place an imagi-

nary phone call. "Whom shall we call?" the parent begins. "How about Uncle Jim?" After a brief conversation with Uncle Jim, the parent hands the telephone to the child and says, "He wants to talk to you." The child may shyly murmur "hi" and then "bye," or just hold the receiver silently. No matter, the parent takes the phone back and ends the conversation. Over time, a toddler will learn from these demonstrations and find a way to become involved. Perhaps the child will recite the names of other people in Uncle Jim's family, wanting the parent to talk to each one in turn. Maybe the child will designate, with a single word, a topic to be discussed by the parent. "Doggie" might mean "talk about Uncle Jim's dog;" "roni" might refer to the macaroni the child spilled last week at Uncle Jim's house.

Parents and toddlers can also conduct imaginary phone conversations with two phones. Since the child needs to hold up one end of the conversation, these calls tend to be very short. "Hello," the parent might begin. "Do you want to go for a walk?"...(The child nods yes.)..."You do? Okay, bring me your shoes and I'll put them on. Then we'll go for a walk. Bye-bye..." Or the parent might hold a doll and speak for it. "Hello, this is Kermit the frog. Remember me? I'm green and I can sing." (The child smiles knowingly.) "Do you have Cheerios at your house? I just love Cheerios." (The child giggles.) "Will you get some Cheerios for me?" (The child drops the phone and runs off in the direction of the Cheerios box.)

Some conversational games can reflect the fears of one-year olds, for as children develop imaginary fears, it is helpful to talk about them. Probably the best example with toddlers is doctor play. Typically, the children have learned to fear visits to the doctor and their fears are heightened by what they imagine the doctor is going to do. Playing with a doctor kit allows these

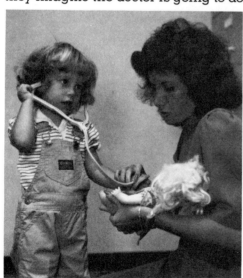 

worries to come out in the open and fears can be reduced to manageable proportions.

For example, one-year olds sometimes are afraid to let the doctor look in their ears. Even though no pain is involved, the feel of the instrument is peculiar and the closeness of the doctor's face is unnerving. Picking up the otoscope from the doctor kit, or some similar instrument, the parent might begin a pretend examination. "Now, let me look at your finger (this is not likely to threaten the child) . . . Hmmmm, I see your fingernails are growing very nicely." Moving up to the child's face, the parent can check out the tip of the child's nose and then the ears. "I have to look way inside your ears to see if there are any germs," the parent might explain, "Kind of tickles, doesn't it?" Such explanations may seem clearly over the child's head, but they still help children cope with the intrusiveness of a physical examination. In the same way parents can model pretending to look in a child's mouth, taking the child's temperature, or checking the child's heartbeat.

With little or no encouragement, older toddlers often assume some version of the doctor role. If they wish, parents can direct the play toward a frightening area by asking the child-doctor to perform a specific action. Requesting a shot, for example, and then helping the child give one to the parent, is a good way to demonstrate the use of a toy hypodermic needle. "Oh, that didn't hurt at all," the parent can say with evident relief. "It was just a pretend shot."

Doctor play, like the other pretend themes we have discussed in this chapter, involves complicated ideas for a one-year old. Sometimes the children will watch their parents play out a scene without making any effort to participate. In fact, the parents may feel they are playing virtually by themselves. Eventually, however, the children will pick up the idea and join in. Through words or gestures, they choose a role that pleases them and a pretend game emerges where both partners play an active part.

\*      \*      \*

Throughout this final section of *One to Two Years* we have been looking at the different ways in which parents and children can play and learn together. In this chapter our focus has been on playing with words. We have recognized that once a child is interested in words, all forms of parent-child play are enhanced by conversation.

Books provide a powerful way to generalize first words and to expand on early phrases. Although there are many different pictures in each book, there is also a high degree of repetition. As parents and children reread books together, they search out familiar pictures in a delightful version of hide and seek. At the same time, each new reading of a book provides an opportunity to learn new words and make new discoveries. Older toddlers frequently begin to appreciate a simple story line in picture books so that reading a book turns into an imaginary experience.

An innate capacity for pretending peeks through in many aspects of toddler play. Parents use toys and playthings to support this initial pretending, but the essential ingredient is their language. Imaginary themes are introduced and feelings of fantasy built up through language. By concentrating on the fun of imaginary play, parents stimulate language in a natural way. Their one-year olds are free to participate without talking, but eventually they will join in the conversational play as they learn to speak.

# Suggested Activities

## *Playing With Books*

When toddlers first get interested in looking at the pictures in a book, they often focus their attention on one or two favorite objects in each book. Reading resembles a game of "Peek-a-Boo." Your child will quietly turn the pages of a book until, there is a favorite image. Parents can hold the book in a way that allows them to share these moments of excitement with their child.

Toddlers are more interested in reading books when they turn the pages. You can give your child a feeling of control over reading. Instead of asking her to label the pictures, or labeling every picture for her, wait until she points to a picture. Then respond to her initiative by labeling the picture.

Toddlers like to label pictures, but they also like to listen to you tell them about the pictures. Listening skills are just as important in language development as speaking skills. One way to encourage both listening and speaking skills is to hesitate before you say certain words. Give your child a chance to finish the sentence for you. "Look at this big dog," you might say. "She goes . . . ." Then, if your child does not respond, you can finish the sentence and continue your reading.

One of the most popular kind of books among toddlers is a photo album. Your child will enjoy labeling family members and hearing you retell memorable experiences. You also can create your own picture book by putting magazine pictures in a photo album. Many children like books of animal pictures. Your child may also like a book that shows food, vehicles, or "Sesame Street" characters.

One-year olds also like books that have parts which can be touched and manipulated. A counting book that has real objects to count, a scratch and sniff book, a book with movable, velcro-backed pieces, a book with sturdy pull tabs — these specialty books combine the fun of reading with the excitement of making something happen.

Most young toddlers would rather talk about the pictures in a book than read the storyline. As your child gets older, she may show interest in listening to a story that accompanies the pictures. Even at this point, it is often best to paraphrase the actual words. Tell the story in your own words, adjusting it to fit your child's attention span.

Reading with toddlers is not limited to books. Since you and your child are really looking at pictures, any interesting picture provides a chance for "reading." These pictures are everywhere — hanging on the wall, on billboards and posters, and most of all on television. Many parents enjoy watching television with toddlers and helping them identify the pictures that flash by on the screen. Programs designed for preschoolers are stimulating for one-year olds when parents are available to "read" the pictures.

## Conversational Play

With help from their parents, toddlers are beginning to act out a variety of pretend themes. Gradually these imaginary situations are elaborated through language, and the high point comes in the conversation that parents and children share. The following are some of the most popular themes for conversational pretending.

Pretending to eat is a universal favorite. As your child's understanding of language grows, you can introduce more dialogue into the play. For example, Snoopy, while pretending to drink from a cup, can also be enjoying "dogfood kool-aid." In turn, each of the family members can try their favorite flavor of kool-aid, and as the one-year old mixes these drinks, his parents will enrich the pretending with their questions and comments.

Another early fantasy theme is "going to work." In preparation for his pretend departure, remind your child to put air in his tires. You can extend the fantasy theme by asking questions: "Need any gas?" "Where're you going today?" "Did you get your lunch?" Toddlers typically leave for work on their wheel toys; however, your toddler may also enjoy using a stationary steering wheel. If your child likes to play with a steering wheel toy, put some popcorn in the glove compartment. It helps to have something to munch on a long trip.

Pretending to talk on the phone is a natural theme for conversational play. When you have a question to ask your one-year old, place an imaginary call. "Ring, ring — your telephone is ringing Robby. Better answer it." Then proceed to ask your question:

"Hello, is this Robby? . . .

I'm going for a walk around the block. Do you want to come too? . . . . .

You do? Okay. Bring your coat and your teddy bear. I'll get the stroller . . . . .
Bye, bye."

 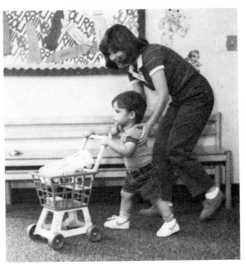

If your toddler enjoys shopping trips to the mall, organize similar trips at home. Pushing a stroller or toy shopping cart, you and your child can travel from department to department (room to room), selecting items that catch your eye. Perhaps you can pick out items that will be used later in the day: a can of soup for lunch, some toys for bathtub play, a record that can be listened to later. This is also a good way to "discover" toys that have been put up for a while because the child stopped playing with them: "Oh look, here is the wind-up mouse that Grandma gave you — let's buy that and take it home."

Many one-year olds develop a fear of the doctor. A doctor kit is an excellent toy for playing out these fears. Parents can help their toddlers by guiding them through an examination: "Doctor, could you look in my mouth please — it hurts . . . . Do you want me to keep this thermometer in my mouth?" Often it is useful to simply talk about the various instruments as you and your child handle them. Although your child will not fully understand your explanations, this kind of conversation helps a toddler accept medical procedures. And while it is certainly no fun to be sick, it is quite a lot of fun to pretend to be sick.

# Chapter 12
# MAKING FRIENDS THROUGH PLAY

| Mother: | "I've invited a friend over for Dahlia." |
|---|---|
| Father: | "Great. They'll have a fine time. Probably discuss their favorite pacifiers, or maybe they'll talk about the relative merits of disposable diapers." |
| Mother: | "Oh, don't be silly. Dahlia and Timothy really do play with each other." (The doorbell rings) "Here they are now." |
| Timothy's Mother: | "I hope we're not too early. Timothy couldn't wait." |
| Mother: | "No, come right in. Dahlia's all set to go. (By now the two toddlers have crept up to each other and are happily tugging at each other's shirt.) |

In this section of the book the emphasis has been on parent-child play. We have looked at the ways in which parents share ideas with their toddlers, adding to the fun and increasing the sophistication of their child's play. With the help of their parents, children learn new ways to manipulate, rearrange, and combine toys and other objects. Names and labels are learned by reading books and looking at pictures. Most significantly, as parents introduce pretend ideas, one-year olds become aware that play can be based on an imaginary theme, and they begin to see how imaginary play is constructed with language.

Parent-child play is indeed stimulating for one-year olds. At the same time, it strengthens the bond of attachment between parents and children. A special kind of friendship is promoted. In fact, as parents play with their one-year olds, they provide a model of how friends play together. They demonstrate in a ball game, the back and forth character of play: "first your turn, then my turn." In block play, they demonstrate how friends cooperate to build something in common. By accepting an invitation to play, they help children learn the value of being assertive. They may even let themselves be bossed around in play by a one-year old. On the other hand, parents encourage their children to accept the necessity for compromises in play situations. This is especially true when parents help a child understand that the play must end for a while.

Obviously these principles of friendship are not learned overnight, but a foundation can be established during the toddler year. In this final chapter, we will see how play, as the medium of friendship, is extended to a wider and wider circle of friends. In a sense, a toddler's play experience with parents provides a bridge to these new relationships with other adults, older children, and toddler peers.

# Making Friends With Other Adults

One-year olds are overcoming their earlier fear of strangers, although they may still be frightened of visitors who look especially strange to them. If these adults remain friendly without being intrusive, the children will usually make up with them eventually. One-year olds are reassured when adults smile and talk to them, but are leery of adults who demand hugs and kisses or who bombard them with questions. Many adults, of course, have a favorite routine for winning over a young child once the initial ice is broken. They may cover their eyes with their hands, then open them slowly and say "peek" in a squeaky voice. They may start a finger moving in a circle, then—buzzing like a bee—move it closer and closer to the child's belly button. Or perhaps they may do a simple magic trick, such as finding a penny behind the child's ear or pretending to pull off and then reattach one of their own fingers.

The most straightforward way for adults to make friends with one-year olds is to offer them interesting objects. The children do not comprehend many of the verbal formulas for communicating friendliness, but handing them a toy is a gesture they understand. In fact, one-year olds frequently signal a desire to make friends by giving an object to a visiting adult, as if to say, "Here's something for you. Do you have anything for me?" As they get older and bolder, the children may actually appropriate objects that belong to a strange adult. When the visitor puts down a purse or hat, the child reaches out to explore it.

Rather than stop the children, parents can use this curiosity to further friendship. They might remind the children that permission is needed, and then help the children do the asking. "Would it be all right if Matthew tried on your hat and looked in the mirror?" "Michelle is very interested in your purse. Do you have anything in your purse she could look at for a few minutes?" Parents, of course, need to treat each situation separately and decide how to phrase their requests delicately. In most instances, however, adults are more than happy to share their possessions temporarily with a one-year old.

With older one-year olds who can follow a conversation, an effective way for adults to begin is with a play routine. An adult, for instance, may take out a mirror and comb and talk to the child's stuffed animal. "Oh, Teddy, you want to borrow my mirror? You need my comb? Oh, all right, but hold on tight." In short order, the toddler will get interested in the play and forget about being shy.

One-year olds also enjoy meeting adults outside the home. Sitting securely in the seat of a grocery cart, they may suddenly greet a passing stranger. Walking in the mall, they may share a brief encounter with a fellow window shopper. Given repeated experiences with the same adults and a chance to make contact by exchanging objects, one-year olds develop definite friendships with clerks in stores, adults at church, and neighbors.

An environment with many possibilities for making friends is a parent's workplace. Secure in the knowledge that a parent is nearby, children can watch a variety of new adults with an intriguing assortment of novel objects. Over time, these faces become familiar and the objects that surround them become the focus of exploration and friendly interaction.

# Making Friends With Other Children

Toddlers play with older children and teenagers in the same way they play with adults. They explore objects with them, play with toys and books, and share physical games. Like adults, these older children are able to adjust their play to fit the interests of a one-year old. In some ways, they are even better players than adults because they are more interested in the toys that appeal to one-year olds. A preadolescent who regularly baby-sits may be a favorite companion.

One-year olds also want to make friends with children who are only a few years older. These preschool children will sometimes include younger children in their play. Often, however, their play is very boisterous, and the running and chasing games prove too much for the toddler. One-year olds are left standing on the sidelines, valiantly trying to imitate bits and pieces of the fast-paced play they are watching.

When playing with a group of children, a mixed age group offers many advantages for one-year olds. There may be children old enough to play individually with a toddler, or children who have sufficient leadership skills to include toddlers in group pretending. There may be other children who are close enough in age to serve as models for one-year olds. Sometimes a mixture of ages results in older children lording it over younger ones and dominating their every move. But if the age range is broad and play is monitored by adults, a mixed age group can encourage cooperation.

Despite the potential in mixed age groups, many one-year olds are grouped with peers at day care centers, church classes and play groups. Traditionally, it was thought that the children did not play very well together in this kind of situation. Episodes of peer play seemed sporadic and likely to end up in a tussle over some toy. More experience with groups of one-year olds, and more careful observation, has revealed that this picture is not altogether accurate. While it is true that one-year olds sometimes fight loudly over toys, it is almost as common for them to give toys to each other. Even when they are not playing together, they spend a good deal of time watching and imitating each other. In fact, the level of interaction and sharing is surprisingly high in a group of one-year olds who have played together for months and know each other well.

We suspect that a critical variable in increasing the peer play of one-year olds is the attitude of parents and other adults. Usually, adults adopt one of two roles when supervising a group of toddlers. Either they play directly with the children, taking the role of a stimulator, or they let the children play by themselves as long as they are not fighting. The alternative that is often overlooked is for the adults to act as facilitators of peer play, to help one child make contact with another. Perhaps by looking for opportunities to help toddlers play with each other, adults can promote a higher level of social interaction.

As parents become more attuned to the possibilities for peer interaction, they can also make changes in the physical environment. There are no hard and fast rules for designing a toddler play environment, but we have certain clues. One-year olds interact more and share toys better when the toys are oversize. A toddler slide is a good example. It is large enough to be shared easily and actually is more fun when used by a group of one-year olds. The children learn by watching each other and then imitating.

There are several other common situations in which large toys lead to imitative, parallel play. Older toddlers enjoy sharing a bathtub or climbing in and out of a crib. A small group may start a game by taking turns jumping off a hassock or a porch step. Ultimately, we will need to manufacture more

of these oversize toys for groups of one-year olds: a busyboard that is big enough for several children to operate simultaneously, a large stacking toy that invites a group effort, wheel toys that have steering wheels, horns and seats for more than one child.

According to several studies, toddlers are also drawn to each other when there are no toys at all. With only a few objects to explore, the children get involved in imitating each other's body movements and facial expressions. They play "peek-a-boo" and chase each other. While adults would not want to offer one-year olds an environment without toys, they can encourage this kind of play in the form of group songs. The children may not be able to sing along very well, but they can join in by moving to the music and making appropriate gestures.

> We clap, clap, clap our hands,
> Clap our hands together.
> We wave, wave, wave our arms,
> Wave our arms together.

Adults who want to try group songs with one-year olds can buy a children's record to get started and then use their own creativity to put additional fingerplays, nursery rhymes and exercises to music.

By observing the interaction patterns of toddlers, we will discover other clues for facilitating peer play. In a home situation, parents can watch the play for a while in order to identify patterns and then introduce appropriate modifications. Allison's mother, for instance, noticed that Allison and her friend, Peter, spent their time chasing each other in a circle—out of the kitchen into the dining room, around the hall and back into the kitchen. Instead of restricting their running, she decided to slow them down by creating "way" stations along the route. She placed a bell that could be pulled on the dining room door frame, a bean bag chair in the dining room for climbing and jumping, and a basket of hardware odds and ends in the kitchen. As the youngsters made the circuit, they frequently stopped at one of the stations, and the play went along at a leisurely pace for a surprisingly long time.

# Handling Conflicts

Peer play between toddlers does not always proceed without conflict. Between the ages of one and two, children become capable of hurting each other intentionally, and intervention is a must. Adults often remind the children who are acting aggressively that it hurts to be hit or bitten. In addition, toddlers can be helped to understand the consequences of aggression by giving attention to the child who has been hurt. Then both aggressor and victim can be encouraged to make up. Perhaps they can be induced to follow a parent's lead and touch each other. Although one-year olds have a limited ability to solve interpersonal conflicts verbally, they do understand conciliatory body language. Parents can demonstrate this way of making amends themselves whenever an occasion arises. "Ooh, right in Mommy's eye," a parent might exclaim when her child accidentally pokes her with an elbow. "Kiss it so it'll be all better."

Some one-year olds develop a regular habit of pinching or biting their peers. Watching these children, it is hard to avoid the conclusion that their attacks are designed to get attention. Those whom they pinch and bite most often seem to be the children they most like. Naturally, this method of initiating play is unacceptable, and it can be very embarrassing for the parents of the pinchers and biters. Nevertheless, such behavior is not unusual among one-year olds. Many children go through at least a brief period in which they experiment with aggressive tactics, seeing if they will lead to interesting social encounters.

Looking for a quick solution, parents sometimes choose to retaliate in kind, a pinch for a pinch and a bite for a bite. The rationale given by these parents is that they want their children to realize that pinching and biting hurts. From the child's point of view, however, the lesson that is learned may be quite different: it is all right to bite and pinch as long as you are bigger and stronger. For parents who do not wish to model aggressive behavior, the alternative is to monitor peer play closely and to intervene every time the child pinches or bites. This approach, although it requires continuous effort, helps children learn in a positive way that biting and pinching will not be accepted.

Finally, let us close with a word about child care. We can be sure that, in the years ahead, an increasing proportion of toddlers will be placed in some kind of child care. It is safe to assume that the children will adjust well to this peer group setting, particularly as we become more knowledgeable about how to structure their environment. At the same time, we should not lose sight of the fact that it will be difficult for some one-year olds to go into a group situation. Separation fears can be expected, especially if children have spent a good part of their first year at home. The children may realize that their parents will return to pick them up, but this does not take away from the unpredictability of their day with substitute caregivers. Who will protect and reassure them in times of trouble? How will the substitute caregivers react to their moods and feelings? Until the children can answer these questions, the child care environment will seem foreboding.

Parents also look for the answers to these questions when they choose a child care environment. They want to find sensitive, loving caregivers, who will help children feel more secure in a group situation. We would suggest that parents also look for adults who are good at facilitating peer group play. Adult attention is at a premium in a child care setting, and the children look to each other for companionship and emotional support. Although peer group interaction is just beginning with one-year olds, we believe that caregivers who stimulate this kind of play will make life happier for the children in their care.

# Making Friends With Pets

In this chapter we have talked about how toddlers make friends. They make friends with aunts and uncles, friends of the family, baby sitters, teachers and children of all ages. Some of their best friends, though, are family pets.

One-year olds can be rough on pets, and sometimes pets are too temper-mental to be trusted with young children. As the photographs below illustrate, however, most of the time toddlers and family pets are mutually attracted to each other.

# SUGGESTED READINGS

## For Children

Brown, Margaret Wise. *Goodnight Moon* (New York: HarperCollins, 1947).

Cunningham, Ed. *Hop Like a Bunny, Waddle Like a Duck!* (New York: Western, 1987).

Dunn, Judy and Phoebe. *The Animals of Buttercup Farm* (New York: Random House, 1981).

Hill, Eric. *Spot's Birthday Party* (New York: Putnam, 1982).

_____. *Spot's First Walk* (New York: Putnam, 1981).

_____. *Where's Spot?* (New York: Putnam, 1980).

Kahn, Peggy. *Did You Ever Pet a Care Bear?* (New York: Random House, 1983).

## For Parents

Brazelton, T. Berry. *Toddlers and Parents* (New York: Doubleday, 1989).

_____. *To Listen to a Child* (Reading, Massachussetts: Addison-Wesley, 1986).

Cass-Beggs, Barbara. *Your Baby Needs Music* (New York: St. Martin's Press, 1980).

Leach, Penelope. *Your Baby and Child* (New York: Alfred A. Knopf, 1989).

Mack, Alison. *Toilet Learning* (Boston, Massachussetts: Little, Brown, 1983).

McDermott, John. *The Complete Book on Sibling Rivalry* (New York: Putnam, 1987).

Sparling, Joseph, and Lewis, Isabelle. *Learning Games for the First Three Years* (New York: Walker and Company, 1979).

# INDEX

# Parenting and Childcare Books
# from Newmarket Press

**Baby Massage**
*Parent-Child Bonding Through Touching*
Amelia D. Auckett; Introduction by Dr. Tiffany Field

A fully-illustrated, practical, time-tested approach to the ancient art of baby massage. Topics include bonding and body contact; baby massage as an alternative to drugs, healing the effects of birth trauma; and massage as an expression of love. Includes 34 photographs and drawings, a bibliography, and an index. (128 pages; 5 1/2" x 8 1/4"; $9.95 paperback)

**How Do We Tell the Children?**
*A Step-by-Step Guide for Helping Children Two to Teen Cope When Someone Dies—Updated Edition*
Dan Schaefer and Christine Lyons; Foreword by David Peretz, M.D.

This invaluable book provides straightforward language to help parents explain death to children from age two through teens. It includes insights from psychologists, educators, and clergy. Special features include a 16-page crisis-intervention guide to deal with situations such as accidents, AIDS, terminal illness, and suicide. "Parents need this clear, extremely readable guide. . . highly recommended." (*Library Journal*) (192 pages; 5 1/2" x 8 1/4"; $18.95 hardcover; $10.95 paperback)

**How to Shoot Your Kids on Home Video**
*Moviemaking for the Whole Family*
David Hajdu

The perfect book for the video-age family and classroom from the editor of *Video Review*. Offers parents and teachers a lively, user-friendly look at making wonderful home videos. Includes eleven ready-to-shoot scripts, clear photographs, and an index. (208 pages; 7 1/4" x 9"; $10.95 paperback)

**In Time and With Love**
*Caring for the Special Needs Baby*
Marilyn Segal, Ph.D.

From a psychologist and mother of a handicapped daughter, sensitive, practical advice on care for children who are physically handicapped, developmentally delayed, or constitutionally difficult. Topics include developing motor skills; learning language; developing problem-solving abilities; and interacting with siblings, family members, and friends. Includes fifty photographs, six resource guides, a bibliography, and an index. (208 pages; 7 1/4" x 9"; $21.95 hardcover; $12.95 paperback)

## Lynda Madaras Talks to Teens About AIDS
*An Essential Guide for Young People—Updated Edition*
Lynda Madaras; Forewords by Linda Levin, M.D., and Constance Wofsy, M.D.

Written for parents, teachers, and young adults ages 14 through 19, this valuable book describes with honesty and sensitivity what AIDS is, why teens need to know about it, how it is transmitted, and how to stay informed about it. Includes drawings, a bibliography, and a resource guide. (128 pages; 5 1/2" x 8 1/4"; $16.95 hardcover; $7.95 paperback)

## Mothering the New Mother
*Your Postpartum Resource Companion*
Sally Placksin

This all-in-one resource guide covers everything from homecare options, help for breastfeeding problems, and workplace negotiation strategies, to adjusting to full-time motherhood, postpartum depression, and hiring a doula. Each chapter is filled with practical suggestions; hands-on solutions; and an invaluable listing of the newsletters, books, hotlines, videocassettes, support groups, services, and caregivers available to the new mother. Includes checklists, planning sheets, an index, and resource guides. (352 pages; 7 1/4" x 9"; $15.95 paperback)

## My Body, My Self
*The What's Happening to My Body? Workbook for Girls*
Lynda Madaras and Area Madaras

The companion book to *The What's Happening to My Body? Book for Girls*, this workbook/diary encourages girls ages 9 to 15 to explore their feelings about their changing bodies. Everything affected by the onset of puberty is covered, from body image, pimples, and cramps, to first periods, first bras, and first impressions. Includes quizzes, checklists, exercises, and illustrations. (128 pages; 7 1/4" x 9"; $9.95 paperback)

## My Feelings, My Self
*Lynda Madaras' Growing-Up Guide for Girls*
Lynda Madaras with Area Madaras

For preteens and teens, a workbook/journal to help girls explore their changing relationships with parents and friends; complete with quizzes, exercises, letters, and space to record personal experiences. Includes drawings and a bibliography. (160 pages; 7 1/4" x 9"; $9.95 paperback)

## Raising Your Jewish/Christian Child
*How Interfaith Parents Can Give Children the Best of Both Their Heritages*
Lee F. Gruzen, Forewords by Rabbi Lavey Derby and the Reverend Canon Joel A. Gibson

This pioneering guide details how people have found their own paths in Jewish/Christian marriages, and how they have given their children a solid foundation to seek their own identity. Includes a bibliography and an index. (288 pages; 5 5/16" x 8"; $10.95 paperback)

### The Ready-to-Read, Ready-to-Count Handbook
*How to Best Prepare Your Child for School—A Parent's Guide*
Teresa Savage

A step-by-step guide that shows how to teach preschoolers basic phonics and numbers. Over 60 phonetic learning exercises, 35 games, homemade flashcards, 24 assignments, and a series of cartoons encourage a tension-free, fun-filled environment while your child develops skills in motor ability, logic, listening, and comprehension. Includes a bibliography, an index, and reference lists. (272 pages; 5 5/16" x 8"; $11.95 paperback)

### Saying No Is Not Enough
*Raising Children Who Make Wise Decisions About Drugs and Alcohol*
Robert Schwebel, Ph.D.; Introduction by Benjamin Spock, M.D.

Widely praised as the first book to present a complete program on how to empower children to defend themselves against drugs, this step-by-step guide shows parents and counselors how to help kids develop the self-confidence and skills necessary to make life-protecting decisions about drugs and alcohol. "Wise and wondrously specific...a solid parental manual." (*Kirkus Reviews*) Includes a bibliography and an index. (256 pages; 5 5/16" x 8"; $18.95 hardcover; $10.95 paperback)

### The Totally Awesome Money Book for Kids (and Their Parents)
Adriane G. Berg and Arthur Berg Bochner

For young readers from ten to seventeen, this fun, fact-filled guide uses quizzes, games, riddles, stories, and drawings to teach the basics of saving, investing, borrowing, working, taxes, and more. Includes illustrations, a bibliography and a glossary. (160 pages; 5 5/16" x 8"; $18.95 hardcover; $10.95 paperback)

### The What's Happening to My Body? Book for Boys
*A Growing Up Guide for Parents and Sons—New Edition*
Lynda Madaras with Dane Saavedra

Written with candor, humor, and clarity, here is much-needed, but hard-to-find information on the special problems boys face during puberty. It includes chapters on the body's changing size and shape, hair, perspiration, pimples, and voice changes; the reproductive organs; sexuality; female puberty; and more. "Down-to-earth, conversational treatment of a topic that remains taboo in many families." (*The Washington Post*) Includes drawings, charts, diagrams, a bibliography, and an index. (288 pages; 5 1/2" x 8 1/4"; $18.95 hardcover; $9.95 paperback)

### The What's Happening to My Body? Book for Girls
*A Growing Up Guide for Parents and Daughters—New Edition*
Lynda Madaras with Area Madaras

Selected as a "Best Book for Young Adults" by the American Library Association, this bestselling book provides explains what takes place in a girl's body as she grows up. Includes chapters on the body's changing size and shape; the reproductive organs; menstruation; male puberty; and much more. Includes drawings, charts, diagrams, a bibliography, and an index. (304 pages; 5 1/2" x 8 1/4"; $18.95 hardcover; $9.95 paperback)

**Your Child at Play: Birth to One Year**
*Discovering the Senses and Learning About the World*
Marilyn Segal, Ph.D.

Focuses on the subtle developmental changes that take place in each of the first twelve months of life and features over 400 activities that parent and child can enjoy together during day-to-day routines. "Insightful, warm, and practical...expert knowledge that's a must for every parent." (T. Berry Brazelton, M.D.) Includes more than 250 photographs and a bibliography. (288 pages; 7 1/4" x 9"; $21.95 hardcover; **$12.00** paperback)

**Your Child at Play: One to Two Years**
*Exploring, Daily Living, Learning, and Making Friends*
Marilyn Segal, Ph.D., and Don Adcock, Ph.D.

Hundreds of suggestions for creative play and for coping with everyday life with a toddler, including situations such as going out in public, toilet training, and sibling rivalry. "An excellent guide to the hows, whys, and what-to-dos of play." (*Publishers Weekly*) Includes more than 300 photographs, a bibliography, and an index. (224 pages; 7 1/4" x 9"; $16.95 hardcover; **$12.00** paperback)

**Your Child at Play: Two to Three Years**
*Growing Up, Language, and the Imagination*
Marilyn Segal, Ph.D., and Don Adcock, Ph.D.

Provides vivid descriptions of how two-year-olds see themselves, learn language, play imaginatively, get along with others, make friends, and explore what's around them. It give specific advice on routine problems and concerns common to this age group. Includes more than 175 photographs, a bibliography, and an index. (208 pages; 7 1/4" x 9"; $21.95 hardcover; $10.95 paperback)

**Your Child at Play: Three to Five Years**
*Conversation, Creativity, and Learning Letters, Words, and Numbers*
Marilyn Segal, Ph.D., and Don Adcock, Ph.D.

Hundreds of practical ideas for exploring the world of the preschooler, with sections devoted to conversation, creative play, learning letters and numbers, and making friends. Includes more than 100 photographs, a bibliography, and an index. (224 pages; 7 1/4" x 9"; $16.95 hardcover; $9.95 paperback)

Ask for these titles at your local bookstore or use this coupon and enclose a check or money order payable to:
**Newmarket Press**, 18 E. 48th St., NY, NY 10017.

BABY MASSAGE
____ $9.95 pb (1-55704-022-2)
HOW DO WE TELL THE CHILDREN?
____ $18.95 hc (1-55704-189-X)
____ $10.95 pb 1-55704-181-4)
HOW TO SHOOT YOUR KIDS ON HOME VIDEO
____ $10.95 pb (1-55704-013-3)
IN TIME AND WITH LOVE
____ $21.95 hc (0-937858-95-1)
____ $12.95 pb (0-937858-96-X)
LYNDA MADARAS TALKS TO TEENS ABOUT AIDS
____ $16.95 hc (1-55704-188-1)
____ $7.95 pb (1-55704-180-6)
MOTHERING THE NEW MOTHER
____ $15.95 pb (1-55704-178-4)
MY BODY, MY SELF
____ $9.95 pb (1-55704-150-4)
MY FEELINGS, MY SELF
____ $9.95 pb (1-55704-157-1)
RAISING YOUR JEWISH/CHRISTIAN CHILD
____ $10.95 pb (1-55704-059-1)
THE READY-TO-READ,
READY-TO-COUNT HANDBOOK
____ $11.95 pb (1-55704-093-1)
SAYING NO IS NOT ENOUGH
____ $18.95 hc (1-55704-041-9)
____ $10.95 pb (1-55704-078-8)

THE TOTALLY AWESOME MONEY BOOK
FOR KIDS (AND THEIR PARENTS)
____ $18.95 hc (1-55704-183-0)
____ $10.95 pb (1-55704-176-8)
THE WHAT'S HAPPENING TO MY BODY?
BOOK FOR BOYS
____ $18.95 hc (1-55704-002-8)
____ $9.95 pb (0-937858-99-4)
THE WHAT'S HAPPENING TO MY BODY?
BOOK FOR GIRLS
____ $18.95 hc (1-55704-001-X)
____ $9.95 pb (0-937858-98-6)
YOUR CHILD AT PLAY: BIRTH TO ONE YEAR
____ $21.95 hc (0-937858-50-1)
____ **$12.00** pb (0-937858-51-X)
YOUR CHILD AT PLAY: ONE TO TWO YEARS
____ $16.95 hc (0-937858-52-8)
____ **$12.00** pb (0-937858-53-6)
YOUR CHILD AT PLAY: TWO TO THREE YEARS
____ $21.95 hc (0-937858-54-4)
____ $10.95 pb (0-937858-55-2)
YOUR CHILD AT PLAY: THREE TO FIVE YEARS
____ $16.95 hc (0-937858-72-2)
____ $10.95 pb (0-937858-73-0)

For postage and handling, please add $2.50 for the first book, plus $1.00 for each additional book. For orders of five or more copies, please add 5% for shipping and handling. Prices and availability are subject to change.

I enclose a check or money order payable to **Newmarket Press** in the amount of _____.

Name_____

Address_____

City/State/Zip_____

**For discounts on orders of five or more copies**, contact Newmarket Press, Special Sales Department, 18 East 48th Street, NY, NY 10017; Tel.: 212-832-3575 or 800-669-3903; Fax: 212-832-3629.

YCAP/BOBAD694.QXD